DISCOUNTED LABOUR:
WOMEN WORKERS IN CANADA, 1870–1939

The years between 1870 and 1939 were a crucial period in the growth of industrial capitalism in Canada, as well as a time when many women joined the paid workforce. Yet despite their increasing participation in employment, women faced a difficult struggle in gaining fair remuneration for their work and access to better jobs. *Discounted Labour* analyses the historical roots of women's persistent inequality in the paid labour force. Ruth A. Frager and Carmela K. Patrias discuss how and why women became confined to low-wage jobs, why their work was deemed less valuable than men's work, why many women lacked training, job experience, and union membership, and under what circumstances women resisted their subordination.

Distinctive earning discrepancies and employment patterns have always characterized women's place in the workforce whether they have been in low-status, unskilled jobs, or in higher-status positions. For this reason, Frager and Patrias focus not only on women wage-earners but on women as salaried workers as well. They also analyse the divisions among women, examining how class and ethnic or racial differences have intersected with those of gender. Discounted Labour is an essential new work for anyone interested in the historical struggle for gender equality in Canada.

(Themes in Canadian History)

RUTH A. FRAGER is an associate professor in the Department of History at McMaster University.

CARMELA K. PATRIAS is an associate professor in the Department of History at Brock University.

THEMES IN CANADIAN HISTORY

Editors: Craig Heron and Colin Coates

DISCOUNTED LABOUR

Acknowledgments

We thank Franca Iacovetta, Donna Lightfoot, Lynne Marks, Kate McPherson, and Wayne Thorpe for their many useful comments on an earlier draft of this manuscript. We are especially grateful to Craig Heron for helping us clarify our arguments and for providing detailed editorial advice. Thanks are also due to Barbara Tessman, our copy-editor; Len Husband; Frances Mundy; and the anonymous reviewer at the University of Toronto Press.

We thank the members of our families – Ariela, Benjamin, Don, and Wayne – for their encouragement and their patience. We dedicate this book to our mothers, Anne Frager and Klára Ács Patriász, and the memory of our fathers, Sam Frager and István Patriász.

Contents

© University of Toronto Press Incorporated 2005
Toronto Buffalo London
Printed in Canada

ISBN 0-8020-0828-3 (cloth)
ISBN 0-8020-7818-4 (paper)

Printed on acid-free paper

Library and Archives Canada Cataloguing in Publication

Frager, Ruth A., 1950–
    Discounted labour : women workers in Canada, 1870–1939 /
Ruth A. Frager and Carmela Patrias.

(Themes in Canadian social history)
Includes bibliographical references and index.
ISBN 0-8020-0828-3 (bound)
ISBN 0-8020-7818-4 (pbk.)

1. Women – Employment – Canada – History – 19th century.
2. Women – Employment – Canada – History – 20th century.
3. Sexual division of labor – Canada – History – 19th century.
4. Sexual division of labor – Canada – History – 20th century.
I. Patrias, Carmela, 1950– II. Title. III. Series.

HD6099.F72 2005   331.4'0971'09034   C2005-904568-x

University of Toronto Press acknowledges the financial
assistance to its publishing program of the Canada
Council for the Arts and the Ontario Arts Council.

University of Toronto Press acknowledges the financial
support for its publishing activities of the Government of
Canada through the Book Publishing Industry Development
Program (BPIDP).

RUTH A. FRAGER AND CARMELA PATRIAS

Discounted Labour: Women Workers in Canada, 1870–1939

UNIVERSITY OF TORONTO PRESS
Toronto Buffalo London

Introduction

'When ... for the same labour, females receive less pay, though that labour may be as well, if not better, performed, we are compelled to feel that an aspersion is cast upon our sex,' wrote an anonymous teacher in 1871. Over 130 years later, advocates of pay equity for women are still wrestling with similar issues. Differential earnings of men and women are widely recognized as a problem in Canada today, and hence are carefully tracked. According to Statistics Canada, in 2002, the earnings of women employed full time, year round, were just 71 per cent of those of their male counterparts. Both the popular media and scholarly studies offer a variety of explanations for this gap. They point out that women face discrimination: they are paid less than men even if they are performing the same jobs. Women are confined to low-wage jobs. Women are on average paid less than men, some studies note, because they have less education, training, and work experience, and fewer female than male workers are unionized. Other studies point out that women, who continue to bear more responsibility for child rearing than men, work fewer hours than men. For the historian, these explanations, however well founded, raise more questions than they answer. How and why did women become confined to low-wage jobs? Why has their work been considered less valuable and therefore deserving of less remuneration than men's work? Why have many women lacked the training, job experience, or union membership that would have enabled them to earn higher wages? This historical study of employed women seeks to provide some answers to these questions.

Because distinctive earnings and employment patterns have characterized women workers whether they have been in low-status, unskilled jobs or in careers in the professions, in management, or in administration, the study focuses not only on women wage-earners but on salaried women as well. The years covered, from 1870 to 1939, form a key period in the development of Canada's industrialization and urbanization, the transformations that laid the foundation for the gender division of labour in contemporary society.

This study builds on a wide range of scholarly works, and it is informed by the historiographic debates that have developed as women's history has matured. Some of the early practitioners of women's history tended to look for women whose historical accomplishments might inspire those struggling to promote women's equality in recent times. But concern quickly arose that such an approach might distort our understanding of women's experiences in the past. Although focusing on prominent women helps to correct the many historical accounts that have left women out altogether, historians have increasingly emphasized the need to look at more 'ordinary' women. This approach, 'history from the bottom up,' has transcended the original tendency to focus on middle-class women. Historians have also increasingly recognized the need to examine not only those women who pushed for women's equality in earlier times (sometimes with the aid of male allies) but also to ask why women did not act more consistently or concertedly to alter their situation.

The early historiography, with notable exceptions, tended to minimize differences among women, presuming too many commonalities. More recently some scholars have questioned the notion that the bonds of sisterhood have historically drawn various kinds of women together. Instead, they have been examining the differences among women, asking especially how class and ethnic or racial differences have intersected with those of gender in various historical circumstances.

When we examine the history of employed women in particular, we ask whether middle-class and working-class women joined together in particular circumstances to confront the gender division of labour. Was there a sisterhood that sometimes crossed not only class lines but also ethnic and racial lines? In analysing how key hierarchies have interlocked in particular historical situations, we also ask under what circumstances working-class males and females might have joined together on the shop floor to struggle against harsh working conditions and low pay. Did class solidarity overcome gender and/or ethnic and racial divisions under particular historical conditions?

The division of labour along gender lines is central to our analysis of the late nineteenth and early twentieth centuries, but, in fact, this division predated industrialization. Indeed it predated the arrival of European colonists in North America. Given the large number of Aboriginal nations living in the area that would become Canada, it is difficult to generalize about the patterns and perceptions of gendered labour among them before the arrival of Europeans. Most scholars would agree, however, that whether they belonged to migrant hunting and gathering societies, or to more sedentary agricultural communities, the work of Native North American women differed from that of men. In both types of societies, women bore and raised children and managed the household, while men were primarily responsible for hunting and warfare. In hunting and gathering societies, women also gathered foods and hunted or trapped small animals. In agricultural communities, growing crops was women's work, but men prepared the soil. While men's and women's work thus differed in Native societies, in many cases men's and women's contributions to the group's economy were valued equally. The relatively egalitarian character of certain Native groups, such as the Iroquois Confederacy and the Montagnais-Nascapi people, distinguished them from the European colonists who gradually came to dominate the continent.

European colonists came from patriarchal societies in which men exercised power over women in all areas of life, including the political and economic spheres. Consequently, in the settlements they established, women's work not only differed from men's work but was also valued less. These settlements, in New France in the seventeenth and eighteenth centuries and in British North America in the late eighteenth and early nineteenth centuries, were predominantly rural, based on small-scale farming and artisanal production.

In these settlements, the distinction between men's work and women's work unfolded in a context where the farm family often produced much of the food the family needed, and farm women and men made many items for the family's own use. The extent to which particular family farms were self-sufficient varied greatly, depending on a wide range of factors, including the local availability of various consumer items and the feasibility of growing cash crops such as wheat. The items that the family bought (such as certain kitchen utensils and farm tools) would have been either imported or made locally in small artisanal workshops.

The division of labour on the farm depended in part on how settled and prosperous the particular farm was. On fairly well-established farms, women focused on child rearing and housekeeping, while men focused on work in the fields and heavy outdoor chores. In addition to cooking and cleaning, women generally made many of the family's clothes, grew vegetables, preserved food (by pickling, drying, and making jam), raised a few chickens and cows, churned butter, and made cheese. In pioneer conditions, women made their own soap and candles and sometimes did the spinning and weaving to make their own cloth.

During the harvest, many farm women helped the men in the fields. On farms that were not well off, farm women often had to help with heavy tasks such as chopping trees, moving stones from fields, ploughing, threshing grain, planting, hoeing, and lugging manure. Where farm families were struggling to make ends meet, the husbands often left their farms temporarily to work elsewhere to earn money that the families badly needed; in these cases, the task of running the farms was left to the women. In fact, women were more likely to take on men's work than men were to take on women's work on the family farms. In many cases, notions of feminine domesticity simply did not apply.

Although the available evidence is fragmentary, farm women's work may have been more burdensome than the work of their menfolk, particularly if the farm was not well off. In the 1860s, one male commentator stressed: 'I have known women, in addition to raising a large family, to do the work of the house; attend to the dairy; to all the gardening that was done; to work up all the wool, commencing with clipping it from the sheep, and ending with making it up into wearing apparel, from the socks to the overcoat. The greater part of the work had to be done after baby was put to bed for the night, and while her "lord and master" was snoozing away the evening in the chimney corner, notwithstanding each had shared alike during the day logging, hoeing or harvesting as the case might be.'

Even though women's work was indispensable on farms, their work was not valued as much as men's. Property rights in British North America (with the exception of Quebec) offer the clearest indication of this. Until the 1850s, all of the pre-industrial family farm – including not only the land and livestock but also all the household items such as cooking utensils and linens – belonged exclusively to the male head of the household, regardless of how much work the woman had contributed. A woman's farm labour did not necessarily entitle her to inherit the whole farm when her husband died. Although more work is needed to uncover patterns of inheritance, it seems that while many men left their entire property to their widows, many did not. In English Canada, dower rights, in principle, guaranteed that one-third of the joint property would be used to ensure the widow's livelihood. In practice, however, control over the farm generally passed into the hands of a son, who was obligated to look after his mother's well-being by providing her with bed and board. The widow thus became dependent on her son. In cases where the woman had inherited property at widowhood, she did not have the power to decide what would happen to this property upon her death. In addition, many wills specified that if a widow remarried, she lost all rights to the property in which she had invested her labour during her first marriage.

Daughters' inheritances were generally smaller than sons', indicating that the work that daughters contributed to their parents' farms was valued less than the sons' contributions. In Upper Canada (later Ontario) in the 1840s, for example, a woman who had cared for her sick father for years assumed that she would inherit his farm. When he died without leaving it to her, the woman sued for compensation for her work. But the judge ruled that she was not entitled to compensation because she was just doing her duty.

In Quebec, the law extended greater protection to women's property rights. The male household head exercised control over the family property during his lifetime, but widows were entitled to half of the communal property if there were other heirs. Daughters, moreover, theoretically received an inheritance equal to that of sons. Yet, parents generally left land to their sons, and assumed that their daughters could gain access to land through marriage. In reality, however, the value of the dowry that the daughter received instead of land was frequently very modest by comparison.

Less well documented, but equally suggestive of the fact that women's work was worth less than men's, were wages paid for domestic service, the main income-generating oc-

cupation for women prior to industrialization. Female domestic servants, who usually helped with tasks such as gardening and dairying as well as housekeeping, sometimes
earned less than half of what a hired male farmhand earned
in the same locale and the same period. An important
reason for paying female domestics less than male hired
hands was that a much wider range of employment opportunities existed for men, even in the pre-industrial period.
In addition to farm labour, males could find work in the
lumber industry, in road and canal construction, and, by
the mid-1800s, in railway construction. Boys could also ac-
quire a trade through apprenticeship to local artisans, such
as shoemakers, coopers (who made barrels), and cabinet-
makers, who provided goods and services that farmers could
not produce for themselves.

With a few exceptions, artisanal workshops were male
terrain. Artisans characteristically worked with fairly simple
tools in small workshops often located in their own homes.
The typical artisanal workshop was owned by the master
craft-worker, who made each product from start to finish,
often with the help of a few others – an apprentice or two, a
journeyman, or perhaps one or two sons. Artisans' wives
probably learned something about their husbands' trades
and even helped them at times, which enabled some unusual widows to take over their husbands' workshops. But
such knowledge was acquired informally and did not enjoy
the formal recognition of a learned trade. The artisan's wife
commonly focused on tasks such as child rearing, cooking,
and housecleaning. Her husband's decision to take on a
live-in apprentice or two added to her domestic labour.
Some women did skilled tailoring, making fine clothing for
well-to-do women, and dressmakers and milliners (makers
of women's hats) sometimes even trained apprentices. Yet
their skills tended not to be as highly valued as men's,
and were seen simply as extensions of women's domestic
responsibilities.

Although the historian can uncover assumptions about

the gendered nature of work in the pre-industrial period, employed women were rarely studied at that time. In British North America, the preoccupation with 'the problem of the woman worker' began sometime before the mid-nineteenth century and mounted towards the end of the century as the pace of industrialization grew. Rapid political and economic changes that occurred earlier in western Europe and the United States heavily influenced perceptions of women's roles in British North America. The commercialization of agriculture and the development of industry, as well as the American and French Revolutions, challenged established social relations. The turbulence reached British North America through waves of northward migration from the United States as well as through transatlantic migration. The growth of publishing and improved transportation also helped bring new ideas to the colonies, including ideas about women's work.

In reaction to the turbulence of the world around them, middle-class commentators created a highly idealized vision of the home as 'haven in a heartless world.' As the domain overseen by women, the home would be characterized by values that were the opposite of the values that came to govern relations in the outside world. The male head of the family – who left the home each day to struggle in the competitive, individualistic, and acquisitive industrial economy – needed a place of rest where he would be nurtured and replenished. In contrast to the amoral competitiveness of the business world, the home would be filled with harmony, under the sheltering wings of a pious woman. For Protestants especially, the home would be the centre of religious morality. Christian values would be nurtured there and transmitted lovingly to the next generation. The young would be protected. Creating and maintaining such a haven was to be the full-time occupation of the woman of the home. This was to be her proper place.

In this context, middle-class commentators worried about the appropriateness of factory work for women at a time when there were very few factories in British North America and hence very few women engaged in this type of work. When, in a lecture to the Halifax YMCA in 1856, the Reverend Robert Sedgewick argued that factory work threatened women's delicacy, fragility, and purity, he thereby revealed a great many assumptions about womanhood. His characterization of women is not only sharply at odds with present-day views, but also clearly did not apply to women workers in his own day. Yet such characterizations rang true to the ears of Sedgewick's middle-class contemporaries, whose views of 'proper womanhood' were shaped by the emerging domestic ideology.

At the same time, working-class people had their own reasons for embracing a version of female domesticity. Even if the notion of the angel of the hearth – unsullied by worldly concerns – might not have been so compelling for them, working-class men customarily depended on the services of their wives in and around their homes. In response to the growing numbers of women and children entering the industrial workforce, these men formulated the ideology of the family wage (although they themselves did not use this term). They argued that the male worker's earnings should be sufficiently high so that neither his wife nor his children would have to go out to work. Their efforts to promote this goal were premised partly on protecting women and children from the harsh working conditions that were so common during industrialization. Attempts to reinforce the notion that women's place was in the home also served to counter the threat that women would function as low-wage competitors for jobs. In addition, given the kinds of jobs available to them, many working-class women may well have preferred to embrace domesticity. To some extent, working-class men and women absorbed middle-class notions of female domesticity, especially notions of respectability linked to the role of the male provider with his 'non-working' wife. Yet even though many male workers were unable to earn a family wage, the idealization of the family wage helped perpetuate women's subordination in the paid labour force by ostensibly legitimating lower wages for women. The idealization of the family wage reinforced women's dependence on men financially.

Racial ideology also played a decisive role in shaping the circumstances of women's employment during this period. Until well into the twentieth century the concept of 'race' was widely used to classify the people of Canada. The 1941 census, for example, still listed residents of Canada by 'racial origin.' Some of the largest 'racial' groups were the English, Irish, Scots, Germans, Italians, Poles, Jews, and 'Asiatics.' It is impossible to discern systematic criteria according to which people belonging to these groups were presumed to be different. The 1941 census takers were in part carrying out the legacy of an earlier period, when 'colour' was one basis for classifying Canadians into 'white,' 'yellow,' 'red,' and 'black' 'races.' Yet, even back then, colour did not offer a complete explanation. Why, for example, were Jewish immigrants from Europe classified as a race apart from whites?

The common belief in a racial hierarchy was deeply embedded in Canadian society, even though the criteria for distinguishing between different races were imprecise. Indeed confusion and change characterized both scientific and popular views of race. The science of phrenology offers a good illustration. Until the 1840s, scientists took seriously the notion that 'racial types' could be defined in terms of skull sizes and shapes, including patterns of bumps on people's heads. These head patterns were supposed to convey information such as the 'natural' level of intelligence of a given racial type. These ideas continued to hold sway among the general population long after the mid-nineteenth century. Whatever criteria they used, however, most Canadians assumed that members of a particular race shared distinctive, inheritable characteristics, and that some races were inferior to others. Such conclusions appeared to them to be a matter of common sense. Accordingly, they deemed some 'races' such as 'Slavs,' 'Italians,' and especially 'Negroes' and 'Indians' as being equipped to perform only the most menial forms of labour and felt justified in excluding them from access to skilled jobs. This racist hierarchy privileged those from northern and western Europe, especially the Anglo-Saxons. Next came central and eastern Europeans, who were followed by southern Europeans and Jews; the bottom of the hierarchy was occupied by people of Asian and African origins, as well as indigenous Canadians. Racist ideas combined with ideas of gender and class in complex ways. In very broad terms, the result was that working-class women from the most disadvantaged 'racial groups' faced three interlocking forms of discrimination, based on their sex, their racial classification, and their class position.

As we turn to the examination of women workers in the years between 1870 and 1939, we shall see how these important ideologies interacted with rapidly changing economic developments as the first and second industrial revolutions unfolded, pulling growing numbers of women into paid employment. This ideological climate combined with economic imperatives to fashion the distinctive characteristics of women's employment. As the domestic ideology and the notion of the family wage were being reasserted in many ways, a major disjuncture was developing between the notion of proper womanhood and the reality of increasing numbers of women going out to work. As different groups grappled with this disjuncture, their very reactions helped shape the patterns of women's employment. Some of these patterns persist to this day.

PART I

Image versus Reality

1

Industrial Capitalism and Women's Work

'Z' left school at the age of fourteen to help her family. Her father made a living hauling goods, and her mother supplemented the family's income by taking in boarders. For the first few months after leaving school, Z helped her mother with domestic chores. But although she needed the help, the mother wanted Z to find a better way to earn a living than 'slaveying' for boarders. Z found a job in a candy factory, wrapping chocolate bars, but left after several months because of poor health.

After a short rest, Z found a job in a millinery factory, trimming women's hats. She quickly became skilled at this, and, within the first six weeks, her wages rose from six to nine dollars a week. But she had to leave because the employer 'yelled and swore at the workers so shockingly that Z's nerves gave out.' After resting a week, she found another millinery job but soon left the new job because she was earning only six dollars and had no prospect of advancement. She next found a job in a store, selling women's hats for ten dollars a week, but her health declined again, partly because she found it hard to stand all day long. After recuperating, she decided not to go back to making women's hats because even though she had a talent for this, the trade was characterized by substanstial seasonal unemployment.

Z found the prospect of clerical work more attractive, so one of the family's boarders started helping her learn to type and improve her spelling. The Toronto researcher who investigated Z's case around 1920 concluded that 'as she is the type of girl who can obey orders and carry out routine work well, and as she is likewise faithful and industrious, she has a fair prospect of success up to the point where her limited general education closes the door to further progress on those lines.'

As Z's case reveals, industrialization created new types of paid employment for females. To both Z and her mother, factory work seemed preferable to domestic work, and clerical work seemed better yet. Z's frequent changing of jobs indicates that she was ambitious to find the best possible employment and that the prospects available to her were limited, characterized by low wages, long and irregular hours, and health hazards. Z's eleven-year-old brother would also discover that his job prospects were limited once he left school. But although working-class males and females faced certain common constraints in the world of paid labour, females also encountered gender-based obstacles.

The First and Second Industrial Revolutions

Industrial capitalism fundamentally transformed Canadian society, dramatically altering the very nature of work. In the process, Canada changed from a predominantly rural society based on small-scale, independent commodity production to a predominantly urban one based on the factory system.

By the 1850s, the first industrial revolution was underway. Transportation networks improved dramatically as canals and railways were built, making it more feasible to sell products to larger markets. Steam power was central to this transformation, for steam engines propelled ships and locomotives. Produced by burning coal, steam also powered the new machines that were being developed for the emerging factories. Resource industries such as lumbering and mining expanded, and large saw mills, flour mills, and textile mills developed. A fairly wide range of factories arose, including those manufacturing boots and shoes, clothing, furniture, stoves, and agricultural implements such as reapers and mowers. Yet, in this phase of industrialization, mechanization was still limited. Of greater impact on the organization of production was the gathering together of workers into larger workplaces.

As the early twentieth century dawned, industrial capitalism accelerated, ushering in the second industrial revolution, which extended up to the Second World War. Electricity (often generated from rivers and waterfalls) emerged as the key power source. Mechanization increased dramatically, fundamentally changing almost all industrial sectors. New industries, including steel, automobiles, pulp and paper, and electrical appliances, became prominent. As more efficient methods of administration became increasingly important, large centralized office bureaucracies developed, and offices expanded further to deal with a flood of paperwork.

Urban centres expanded rapidly as industrial growth pulled more people in from rural areas and from abroad to work in factories and other expanding workplaces. From 1891 to 1921, the populations of the two most important industrial cities, Montreal and Toronto, almost tripled, surpassing 615,000 in Montreal and 520,000 in Toronto. Several cities experienced even more dramatic growth rates, and by 1921 the populations of Winnipeg, Vancouver, Hamilton, and Ottawa exceeded 100,000. By then, half the nation's population was classified as urban.

From the late nineteenth century to the end of the period under consideration, the protective tariff facilitated much of this economic growth by reducing competition from imports. Mergers also reduced competition. Although large firms had emerged in some sectors by the 1890s, a series of dramatic mergers in the first dozen years of the twentieth century led to large conglomerates, especially in steel manufacturing, cement manufacturing, and canning. The age of monopoly capitalism had dawned.

Yet industrial development was highly uneven, not only because of dramatic regional variations, but also because the pace of change varied from sector to sector and even within particular sectors. In the late nineteenth century, significant industrial development occurred in the Maritimes as well central Canada. But by the early twentieth century, the nation's industrial heartland centred in Ontario and, to a lesser degree, Quebec, notably in a string of industrial cities extending from Windsor along the Great Lakes to Montreal. Some sectors of the economy industrialized more rapidly than others so that, in the late nineteenth century, new factories co-existed with older forms of production even in the most industrialized parts of the country. During the first industrial revolution, in particular, mechanization had been uneven. But even during the second industrial revolution, characterized by the rise of large corporations, small firms continued to compete with one another in such sectors as clothing and food processing. Frequent economic downturns in the late nineteenth and early twentieth centuries, moreover, reinforced the unevenness of industrial development.

The Reorganization of Work

The rise of industrial capitalism entailed major changes in the organization of work, as employers sought to break up the artisans' traditional control over their trades. This was not simply a question of gathering more workers under one roof so as to manufacture more items to sell to a larger market. Employers strove to make their businesses more competitive and more profitable by cheapening the cost of labour. To do so, they transformed the labour process in two main, interrelated ways, both of which involved the process of deskilling. Employers often increased the division of labour: instead of one or two people making an entire product from start to finish, the steps involved in making that product would be broken down and divided among a group of less skilled – hence less expensive – workers, each of whom would specialize in a particular task. Employers also resorted to mechanization to cut labour costs.

The boot and shoe industry was one sector where the subdivision of labour was already notable by mid-century. By the 1880s, fifty people were involved in the routine production of a boot in Toronto's largest boot and shoe factory. This level of specialization meant increasingly repetitive and tedious work. The craft of shoemaking was dramatically altered through mechanization as well, particularly with the introduction of sewing machines and pegging machines in the 1850s and 1860s. The McKay sole-sewing machine could stitch together as many shoes in one hour as a skilled craft worker could stitch by hand in about eighty hours. This rendered the trained hand-stitcher obsolete. It also meant that the control of the labour process was shifting from the traditional artisan to the employer. Employers deemed this system to be cheaper and more efficient.

As managers coordinated the actions of growing numbers of workers and machines, new rhythms of work formed. Instead of the more natural variations in the pace of work in artisanal workshops, factory labour became highly regimented. Long hours became commonplace, and the pace was often gruelling, as employers sought to maximize the utility of expensive machines. Although the assembly line did not become widespread in this period, those women and men who worked on the line had to keep up with the rapid pace set by the line itself. More commonly, the system of piecework was used to speed up workers. Under this system, instead of paying the worker a set wage per hour, the worker was paid according to the number of items (or parts of items) she or he had produced. Instead of timing average workers, employers frequently set piece rates according to the time required by the fastest workers. When they believed that workers were able to earn too much money under the established rates, employers often reduced piece rates. As factory inspectors emphasized, piecework seriously strained workers' nerves.

Some employers used time and motion studies to speed up workers and to ensure that tasks would be performed in set ways so as to ensure maximum efficiency. For the worker, the result was not only monotonous work but also the risk of what would now be called repetitive strain injuries. A middle-class reformer who disguised herself as a 'factory girl' in order to investigate working conditions, in 1912, captured the monotony of making jelly wafers at a biscuit factory: 'Dab-a-jelly, turn-a-biscuit, dab-a-jelly, turn-a-biscuit, dab-a-jelly, turn-a-biscuit.' Lunch or supper breaks were short, and there were often very few other breaks in the day, even for using the washroom. (These high levels of factory regimentation were cleverly satirized by Charlie Chaplin in his 1936 film *Modern Times*.)

In the late nineteenth century, a rigid system of fines sometimes formed part of the regimentation of factory work. Workers who arrived five or ten minutes late might find their pay docked for the whole morning. In some workplaces, employers docked people's pay for work that they judged to be imperfect, even though such judgments could be subjective and the imperfections might have resulted from problems that were beyond the individual worker's control. In a Halifax textile factory, for example, a weaver received a fine because oil had dripped from the loom onto the cloth, even though oiling the machine was not her responsibility. Talking, singing, and laughing were forbidden in some workplaces, and management used fines to enforce these prohibitions. Employers appear to have fined women and children much more than adult male workers, presumably because the employers viewed women and children as more docile and therefore more likely to put up with the penalties. Some employers also used corporal punishment to discipline child workers, sometimes quite brutally.

Mechanization, together with employers' desire to cut

costs, introduced new hazards into the workplace. Improperly maintained steam-driven equipment could explode. Various kinds of machinery could ensnare fingers and sometimes limbs. The threats to health increased as employers proved reluctant to spend money on proper ventilation and on safety guards for machinery. While tuberculosis was known as the 'tailors' disease' because of its link to the harmful lint and fumes in clothing factories, lung problems related to poor ventilation plagued workers in other trades as well. Lives were shortened and even lost due to job-related diseases and workplace accidents.

Male craft workers resisted the imposition of the factory system – when they could. The dramatic changes in the labour process undermined their income and their pride in their skills. Traditionally, their sense of self-worth – indeed, their very manhood – had been intrinsically bound up with their craftsmanship. But deskilling enabled employers to turn to new sources of cheap labour, particularly women, children, migrants from Canada's rural areas, and immigrants.

Children served as an important pool of cheap labour, particularly during the first industrial revolution. Some, especially those working in textile mills, were only nine or ten years old. While some urban boys plied street trades such as selling newspapers or shining shoes, the intense subdivision of labour in certain sectors in the late nineteenth century enabled a significant number of boys and girls to find factory jobs, often working with light machinery. Over all, fewer girls than boys took up wage earning, for girls often had to help their mothers at home. Parental decisions about whom to send out to work were influenced by the fact that a girl's earning power was commonly less than her brother's. Although the scarcity of historical studies of child labour makes it difficult to generalize, existing studies suggest that, at least in Ontario, employers came to rely less on child labour as factories became more mechanized in the early 1900s.

Employers were sometimes frank about why they employed women. As a cigar manufacturer from London, Ontario, explained in the late nineteenth century, the employment of women 'is more profitable to us or we would not employ them.' He also valued female employees because he believed they were more tractable. 'Women do not go on strike and do not get drunk,' he maintained. A late-nineteenth-century printer advanced similar arguments: 'The proprietor says he likes to have girls because they never ask for a raise of wages, and he can get rid of them some day when he does not need them. They get married.'

Women at Work

Although employers commonly viewed them as cheap labour, most females who went out to work did so because of pressing economic need. For many working-class families in particular, the wages of the male head of the family were simply not enough. At a time when many workers believed that men should bring home a family wage, this ideal did not correspond to reality for most working-class households. In Toronto in 1921, for example, the average annual wage of adult male blue-collar workers constituted only two-thirds of what was necessary to keep a family of five above the poverty line. Hence, secondary wage-earners were necessary, if these families were to cover basic items such as food and rent. In addition, in a period before social welfare measures such as unemployment insurance and socialized medicine, families often needed additional wage earners to help them cope with emergencies resulting from layoffs, sickness, and deaths.

Although some working-class wives and mothers took regular jobs outside the home, most did not, for it was difficult to combine homemaking with going out to work. These 'non-working' women exhaustively strove to stretch the male breadwinners' wages to cover as much as possible. Sometimes assisted by children, they hunted endlessly for food bargains, scavenged the streets and railway tracks for items such as wood and coal, bartered for various items, and scrounged for more. If they could find a small patch of land, even in urban settings, they might grow vegetables or perhaps raise a few chickens. If they produced a surplus of vegetables or perhaps extra baked goods, they sold or traded the surplus to neighbours. Sometimes they took in other people's laundry or mending to earn extra money to make ends meet. Sometimes, like Z's mother, they took in boarders, and this meant that the women had even more domestic work to do, feeding boarders, cleaning up after them, and washing their clothes.

The work of these women was arduous and time consuming, especially when dwellings lacked hot and cold running water and electricity. Although these amenities were becoming more widely available after 1900, the smaller resource towns and new working-class suburbs were slower than large urban centres to obtain these conveniences. Doing laundry without the benefits of indoor plumbing and automatic washing machines meant hauling buckets of water, heating large tubs of water on the stove (without scalding anyone), and soaking, scrubbing, and wringing clothes by hand.

Since wives' work maintaining their homes and stretching the breadwinners' wages was so crucial, families turned for extra wages to sons or daughters in their teens or early twenties, where possible. Given women's generally low wages, it often did not pay to send mothers out to work, especially if they would need to pay for babysitters and carfare to and from the workplace. Many employers who utilized women's labour, moreover, would not employ married women.

For these reasons, women who earned wages or salaries constituted a relatively small proportion of all Canadian women, throughout this period. In 1901, only 16 per cent of the nation's females (age fifteen and older) participated in the paid labour force. The female participation rate climbed slowly in the first four decades of the twentieth century, reaching 22 per cent in 1931 (during the Great Depression) and 23 per cent in 1941 (during the early years of the Second World War). By contrast, the overwhelming majority of males in the same age category went out to work. This wide difference in female and male participation rates meant, of course, that females constituted a minority of those who went out to work. In 1901, only 13 per cent of those in the paid labour force were female. This proportion increased slowly, reaching 17 per cent in 1931 and almost 20 per cent in 1941.

Although these proportions are small by today's standards, the actual number of females in the paid labour force was increasing rapidly. In 1901, approximately 240,000 females engaged in paid labour; by 1921, this number had more than doubled, reaching some 490,000. This figure continued to rise dramatically, reaching about 665,000 in 1931 and 835,000 in 1941. Moreover, the proportion of women in the paid labour force was much higher in urban than in rural areas. By 1921, women constituted 29 per cent of the paid labour force in Toronto and 25 per cent in Montreal, for example, as compared with less than 10 per cent in the heavily rural province of Saskatchewan. According to the census, the women who performed unpaid household labour and various unpaid forms of farm labour were not 'working.' But even in cases where women did earn wages or salaries, they tended to be under-enumerated in certain occupations.

Because the economic development of Canada was so uneven, women had somewhat different choices to make in different regions. Women in Cape Breton's mining towns, for example, found few opportunities for employment in contrast to women in major urban industrial areas. In many small towns, patterns of women's employment depended a great deal on the types of local industries, particularly on the presence or absence of the kinds of industries that typically provided jobs for women.

Homework

Some women, particularly married women, strove to make ends meet by taking in homework from factory owners or contractors. They found it easier to combine this kind of home-based income earning with their domestic responsibilities, particularly if they had young children. Some Maritime women, for example, packed factory-made candy in their homes, and some of Toronto's Italian immigrant women peeled and washed onions in their own homes for the food-processing industry. But the most important source of homework was the garment industry. Contractors in this sector would give out precut pieces of garments to be stitched together in individual homes, particularly in the Montreal and Toronto areas. Census takers tended to underestimate the number of homeworkers in the needle trades, partly because employers were often secretive about these arrangements, as they did not want to be held responsible for their homeworkers' harsh circumstances. The available figures indicate that, at the turn of the century, there were approximately 7,500 women homeworkers in this sector in Ontario and 9,000 in Quebec.

But it was difficult to combine this kind of work with raising a family. Home sewing meant that the family's cramped living quarters had to double as workrooms. While many of the homeworkers in this sector were women, they were often aided by their children. Children as young as five helped pull out basting threads, for example, and ten-year-olds could sew on buttons. Occasionally, men performed homework in this sector as well. Whole families sometimes toiled together in their cluttered kitchens, sewing late into the night.

Wages for homeworkers in the garment industry were extremely low, partly because of the abundant supply of women seeking this work. Isolated from each other and competing for scraps of work, they desperately underbid each other. Factory owners and contractors striving to cut labour costs so as to improve their competitive positions and profitability in the cutthroat needle trades capitalized on the women's desperation. Since contractors paid by the piece instead of paying an hourly rate, the pressure to sew quickly and to keep at it for hours on end was intense. Earnings could be reduced by fines levied for allegedly shoddy work, as well as by the need to pay for items such as thread, scissors, lighting, and fuel. Many homeworkers had to rent or buy their own sewing machines. As they toiled eighteen hours a day during the height of seasonal work, some homeworkers in this industry found it extremely difficult to fulfill their domestic responsibilities.

Nonetheless, homework was common in the needle trades in the late nineteenth century and had not vanished by the start of the Second World War. Yet as the advantages of the factory production of clothing increased in the early twentieth century, homework decreased significantly, thereby posing new dilemmas for working-class women who sought to earn money while staying home with young children.

The Women Who Went Out to Work

Since working-class families requiring secondary wage-earners were reluctant to send wives out to work, the vast majority of females who went out to work were young and unmarried. Most females engaged in paid labour as an interval between leaving school and marrying. Hence the proportion of workers who were female varied dramatically not only according to locale but also according to age. In 1921 and 1931, for example, a little less than one-third of all workers aged 14 to 24 were female. This proportion then declined for 25 to 34 year olds and fell sharply to a mere one-tenth for 35 to 64 year olds. The female labour force participation rate for 20 to 24 year olds reached nearly 40 per cent in 1921 and climbed to over 45 per cent in 1931. The available figures indicate that in 1931 and 1941, only a tenth of the females who went out to work were married.

It would be incorrect to view young, unmarried female income earners as independent women who controlled their own earnings and lived on their own while enjoying freedom from parental control. Most female income earners were embedded in the family economy. Many of these young women lived with their families and contributed all or most of their earnings to their families. Indeed a significant number of them handed their unopened pay envelopes over to their mothers. Many other young women probably retained only a small portion of their pay for their own purposes and routinely handed over the rest. Young women who had left rural families to come to the city to take up paid labour, sometimes lived with surrogate families, often consisting of members of extended families or relatives of former neighbours. Those who lived in 'respectable' boarding houses faced constraints imposed by boarding-house keepers who sought to maintain their reputation for respectability by restricting opportunities for socializing with the opposite sex. Given how difficult it was for female income-earners to earn a living wage, notions of their independence are misleading. These young women may have challenged parental authority to a certain extent by going out to unchaperoned dance halls or taking up the latest fashions (such as bobbing one's hair), but they did not necessarily abandon family loyalties or neglect family obligations. In fact, many took pride in their economic contributions to their families' well-being.

While many women faced limited job opportunities, difficult working conditions, and low wages, they were not simply victims. Like Z, they were active agents in the paid labour force, manoeuvring within sharp constraints to make the most of their limited options. Some obtained a sense of satisfaction from doing their jobs well, even though the jobs could be tedious. Women who went out to work because they and their families needed the money sometimes found

other benefits as well. Many appear to have especially enjoyed the camaraderie with female co-workers, and those
who were looking for male friends, perhaps seeking marriage partners, may have enjoyed mingling with male co-
workers as well. Those who did manage to support themselves
usually took pride in their ability to do so, and, as we shall
see, those who performed white-collar work took pride in
the higher status that this type of work often afforded.

In the rare situations where women possessed scarce skills
and could bring in somewhat better wages, there could be
other important benefits. A study of skilled female textile
workers recruited in the early twentieth century from England for the mills of Paris, Ontario, for example, indicates
the advantages that such women enjoyed. Their greater
earning power, combined with the possibility of lifelong
work in the textile mill, enabled some to escape troubled
marriages and meant that the single women among them
did not necessarily have to marry for economic reasons. In a
town where so many mothers continued to go out to work,
moreover, accommodations, such as flexible employment
hours and commercial laundries providing door-to-door
delivery, developed to facilitate the combination of outside
work with household responsibilities.

Far more often, however, working-class women who had
to support children without the aid of husbands were in a
very vulnerable position, especially because women's jobs
usually paid so little. Aging widows found it difficult to
compete for jobs with young women in their late teens or
early twenties. And, of course, it was hard to combine income earning with household responsibilities, particularly
if the children were young. Widows and deserted wives
constituted a small but significant group of female income-
earners who confronted particular hardships.

Factory Work

The manufacturing sector was an important source of jobs,
especially for women who lacked the language skills or the

formal education required for white-collar work. Of all females in the paid labour force in 1901, almost 30 per cent were concentrated in factory work, a proportion that declined to a low of 13 per cent in 1931. This decline needs to be seen in relation to the rapid growth of the white-collar workforce in the early twentieth century. Within manufacturing, females represented a significant proportion of workers – roughly one-quarter from 1891 to 1911 and around one-fifth from 1921 to 1941. Women in factories tended to concentrate in a few areas: the textile, clothing, boot and shoe, food-processing, and tobacco industries. The highest proportion of female workers was in the clothing industry: in 1901 and 1911 three-quarters of the workers in that industry were female. This sector employed more women than any other manufacturing sector at the turn of the century.

These women typically earned little. In the late nineteenth and early twentieth centuries, many factory women did not make enough to be economically self-sufficient, let alone support elderly parents, young children, or an ailing husband (or other partner). Those who managed to eke out a living wage for themselves usually remained poor and seldom had savings for unemployment, illness, or old age. Female income-earners typically made far less than males, especially in manufacturing. Women's annual incomes averaged 54 per cent of men's in 1921 and 60 per cent in 1931; in manufacturing, the figures were only 43 per cent and 44 per cent respectively. Throughout the period under consideration, factory women earned roughly half as much as men. With so many jobs off limits to females, women workers' intense competition for the available 'women's work' helped to keep their pay low. Yet they still earned less when they had the same jobs as men.

The Gender Division of Labour

Even though women workers constituted an important pool of cheap (and reputedly docile) labour, women were not pulled into the paid labour force indiscriminately. Many jobs were off limits to women because of the ways in which the prevalent gender ideology intertwined with men's material self-interest, as employers, as workers, and as heads of families.

The gender division of labour was commonly seen as natural, fixed, and immutable. Some industries were deemed totally unsuitable for women. Even where they found work, they usually encountered a distinct differentiation between 'women's' and 'men's' work and thus seldom competed directly with men for jobs. To contemporaries, these distinctions seemed to reflect common sense. Women seemed incapable of heavy work, such as making steel, cutting down trees, or mining coal. Women's jobs were generally regarded as an extension of work that women had traditionally done in the home. They were seen as naturally good at delicate work by virtue of their nimble fingers, their patience, and attentiveness to detail. Beyond this, they were believed to be good at putting up with tedious, repetitious tasks and were often believed to be unsuitable for tasks requiring considerable exercise of individual judgment. They were not seen as skilled workers, nor were they seen as having mechanical ability.

Such 'logic' was, in fact, heavily shaped by customs, indeed stereotypes, rooted in deep beliefs about what constituted 'womanhood' and 'manhood.' At the most basic level, it did not occur to anyone that women could fill men's jobs. Employers would not hire them, and women themselves would not apply because they shared the conventional assumptions that they were by nature unsuited to such work. As a woman who spent years on an assembly line making watches explained succinctly: 'Girls just didn't do men's jobs.' For her, as for so many others, this fact was strongly related to the man's role as family breadwinner: 'Yes, the men were better paid too. We just took that for granted, I supposed because they had families.' A woman who packed cereal for years explained: 'I was still a woman, and I don't believe in taking a man's job.' Thus, in many cases, there was no need to patrol the boundaries of the gender division of labour.

This division of labour was so entrenched that it resulted in certain rigidities. A shortage of women workers in an early-twentieth-century New Brunswick candy factory, for example, did not lead management to hire men to fill women's jobs, even though the shortage limited production and some of the women's jobs paid relatively well.

None of this was inevitable, however. In theory at least, many new factory jobs could have emerged without necessarily being coded as female or male and, in practice, the gender designation of some jobs could change over time and from place to place. Consider the assumption that heavy work was for men. Not only did women perform heavy work on struggling family farms and in working-class households, but the definition of certain jobs as physically demanding – and hence men's jobs – could be arbitrary. In the late-nineteenth-century shoe industry, for example, men and women held different jobs, partly on the grounds that women needed to sit while working whereas men, being physically stronger, could stand. Yet many women in the textile industry, as well as a number of other sectors, worked at tasks that required them to stand for hours on end. Moreover, while some of the machines involved in shoe-making required that the operator stand in order to exert more leverage, a number of shoe-making machines were built in such a way that the operator had to stand – apparently not for any functional reason but rather to define the task as men's work, worth higher pay. Gendered assumptions can clearly be embedded in new technology in ways that disadvantage women. In a historical context where mechanization has eliminated some of the worst forms of backbreaking male labour, we need to think about how men have retained physically demanding elements of certain jobs in order to continue to define them as men's jobs.

The conception of women's factory jobs as simply extensions of their domestic work was similarly problematic. Which jobs did they actually hold in clothing, textile, and food-processing plants? Women had traditionally cooked for their families, but men obtained the main jobs in food processing. In a candy factory, men performed the main tasks in making the candies, while women's 'naturally' nimble fingers were employed simply to dip and decorate candy centres and to pack the boxes. Similarly, at a Quaker Oats factory, men baked the oats while lower-paid women packed the cereal and performed other secondary tasks. The same pattern held in key branches of the garment industry, even though women made most of the clothing for their own families. In these branches, women were confined to jobs as 'finishers,' adding hooks, buttons, and belts. In some cases, women and men performed similar tasks in garment production, but more generally women were confined to the lower-paid jobs that were deemed less skilled. The cutters (who cut out the patterns in the cloth) and the pressers (who ironed each finished garment into shape) were men – the 'aristocrats' of the trade whose jobs were so crucial to the quality of the end product.

The common conception of female workers as less skilled than males is itself problematic. It is difficult to assess the levels of skill in any job objectively and precisely. Some jobs were clearly less skilled than others, and this reality is crucial to the notion of deskilling. A person needs more skill to make a complete coat from start to finish than to sew in coat linings all day long. But assessments have often been shaped by subjective perceptions of what is skilled and what is not, and these perceptions have been shaped by ideological factors. In other words, skill is socially constructed. To analyse the social construction of skill in particular historical circumstances, one needs to examine how common particular skills have been, the types of people who have possessed such skills, the nature of access to various forms of training and experience, and the extent to which groups of workers have been able to defend their claims to particular skills. In the garment industry, for example, women's sewing abilities were demeaned. Sewing skills they had learned from their mothers and performed in their own homes were seen as simply natural to them and evaluated in a context where women's household skills and household labour were generally undervalued.

William Lyon Mackenzie King was right when he observed at the turn of the century that, in the clothing industry, 'the reward for female labour is still greatly at a discount as compared with that of the opposite sex.' In fact, one late-nineteenth-century clothing manufacturer was uncommonly frank when asked what he paid his help. 'I don't treat the men bad, but I even up by taking advantage of the women,' he replied. 'I have a girl who can do as much work, and as good work as a man; she gets $5 a week. The man who is standing next to her gets $11.' He explained that the other 'girls' averaged $3.50 per week and some of them made a mere two dollars. As this example suggests, low wages for women – both when they were doing the same jobs as men and also more broadly – need to be viewed partly in terms of manufacturers' strategies, for some manufacturers deliberately tried to buy off male workers at the women's expense.

The notion that a woman's 'proper place' was in the home ('a man's castle') meant that women who did go out to work were often not viewed as legitimate participants in the paid labour force, even though a significant number of them had no men to support them. Since women were not expected to be self-supporting or supporting dependants, the common presumption was that they were working merely for 'pin money,' for small luxuries. They were also assumed to be temporary workers, employed for a short time before marriage or, if married, working only while their husbands were ill or unemployed. Practices such as paying women less than men for the same work, or laying women off first, were thus based on the assumption that women could not do the work as well as the men who stayed in the trade for years.

In fact, women workers often did leave their jobs. Many did get married. Others withdrew briefly if their mothers or male relatives needed help at home. The relatively few married women who worked outside their homes frequently moved in and out of the paid labour force in a pattern of their own, often regulated by pregnancies. After a baby was weaned, a woman might return to her paid job, only to leave it when the next child was born. As the children grew older and were able to contribute to the family income, a woman might concentrate on her domestic responsibilities, perhaps to return to paid labour only when her children had left home.

Many women changed jobs frequently, particularly if they lacked scarce skills. They might move from one type of factory work to another and from factory work to waitressing or fruit picking and then back to the factories again. Females like Z were responding to the boredom of repetitive work and the difficult working conditions in many workplaces. While employers used high rates of turnover to justify confining women to relatively unskilled, low-wage jobs, this rationale became a self-fulfilling prophecy. The poor jobs encouraged even more transiency and also caused women to hope all the more to be able to leave paid employment upon marriage, thus reinforcing heterosexuality. At the same time, those who faced racist discrimination had less flexibility in moving from one job to another, as did those who tended towards a particular sector for ethnocultural reasons. Those who lived in locales such as mining towns had fewer choices of 'women's jobs' as well.

In any case, it is misleading to think of females as temporary income earners and males as workers who stayed at a job permanently. For women, the interval between leaving school and marrying might last nearly a decade, particularly for working-class females who quit school at age fourteen or fifteen. Female textile workers in Quebec who began work in the early 1900s sometimes continued in these jobs for fifteen years. Nor did the male income earner necessarily devote a lifetime to his job. White-collar males in more prestigious occupations were more likely to fit the image, but many working-class males were relatively transient, particularly if they lacked scarce skills. In the early twentieth century, many non-British immigrant males, in particular, were sojourners who intended to save money while working in Canada and then return home to the Old World. They also shifted frequently from one type of unskilled job to another. Many of the Italian immigrant men who worked for the Canadian Pacific Railway in early-twentieth-century Montreal, for example, did so for less than six months, and a significant number of them spent less than a month at these jobs. Non-immigrant men might also take up jobs temporarily until they found something better, perhaps in a different industry altogether. And, of course, men as well as women faced unemployment (including seasonal layoffs in such a cold climate) that could prod them to switch to other work. Hence we need to question the common perception that women's short-term stint in the paid labour force legitimated confining them to relatively unskilled, low-waged work. Ultimately, there were other powerful forces keeping women's earnings low.

Examples from the unionized shops in Toronto's men's fine clothing industry in 1920 highlight the weakness of conventional rationales. In these cases, the women who did the same work as the men invariably earned considerably less. Sometimes the women did have less experience than the men. Male buttonhole makers, for example, had an average of nineteen years of experience and received an average wage of $36 per week, while female buttonhole makers had an average of only seven years of experience and received an average wage of only $22 per week. Given that one could learn to be a fairly fast and efficient buttonhole maker in far less than seven years, it is doubtful that the discrepancy between men's and women's skills was sufficiently great to warrant such wide pay differentials. Moreover, in a few cases in 1920, women and men performed the

same jobs in these shops, and the women had experience
equal to or greater than the men, yet the women still earned
dramatically less.

Among telegraph workers at the beginning of the twentieth century, the women and men basically did the same
kinds of work, sending and receiving messages in Morse
code. Males, however, usually monopolized the work on
telegraph lines with high volumes of traffic. They, along
with their supervisors, maintained that the female telegra-
phers were less skilled. Yet the men's judgment was clearly
subjective, for it was based partly on the 'musicality' of
operators' transmission styles. Women's Morse code was
allegedly distinctly feminine (reputedly like a woman's
voice), in contrast to men's code, which was rapid, clean,
and unsentimental yet musical. Such subjective judgments
both reflected and reinforced stereotypes of women's inferiority. These judgments were used to legitimate women's
lower pay, as well as to restrict women to telegraph lines
that tended to have lower volumes of traffic. In turn, this
restriction meant that women were shut out of important
experience that would have helped them improve their
skills.

In a sense, women have been the opposite of the legend-
ary King Midas, whose touch turned objects into gold. Because women themselves have been devalued, a woman's
touch has had a negative effect. Women did not simply fill
jobs deemed unskilled: certain kinds of jobs were seen as
less skilled and less remunerative *because* women did them.
And, in circular fashion, the presence of women in devalued jobs reconfirmed notions of women as lacking skill.

Because men were seen as possessing innate mechanical
ability that women allegedly lacked, men were regarded as
better candidates for extensive training and critical on-the-
job experience. In the textile industry, for example, fixing
knitting machines and looms was work reserved for men. In
Paris, Ontario, perceptions of natural mechanical ability
were central to distinguishing between certain women's

and men's jobs in the first half of the twentieth century. Unlike female knitters on the day shift, male knitters on the night shift incorporated the work of the fixers into their own jobs. The men apparently took pride in the mechanical skills that women knitters had not had the same opportunities to develop.

The law could help entrench the gender division of labour. The restriction of mining to men, for example, was legally sanctioned in Ontario in 1890. Statutes banned females from working in bars in Manitoba and as newspaper vendors in Toronto. Although it appears that the legal prohibition of women working in certain occupations was rare, the law could have related ramifications. Some laws were enacted in the name of protecting women from especially dangerous working conditions as well as particularly long hours and night work. Even though these measures were not well enforced, they reinforced the notion that certain jobs were solely for men. Certain kinds of government regulations, such as the Civil Service Commission's classification of job openings by sex, also contributed to this outcome.

Sometimes all these practices were not enough, however, and the boundaries of the gender division of labour had to be policed actively by male workers themselves. Although male unionists sometimes allied themselves with women workers to resist harsh employers, there were instances where male unionists did their utmost to try to ensure that certain jobs would be reserved for men. For craft workers, opposition to female labour stemmed partly from the exclusivist aspects of pre-industrial artisanal traditions. In addition, the defensive actions of these male workers need to be seen in a context where they were often struggling against powerful employers in an era that was profoundly anti-union.

Indeed, employed males, especially working-class males, feared that the employment of women would intensify job competition, thereby allowing employers to undercut wages and hence undermining the men's ability to provide for their families. Often, a man's sense of identity and self-worth, indeed his very notion of masculinity, was bound up with the importance of being the family breadwinner – who could count on his wife's services at home. For blue-collar males especially, the role of the family breadwinner had taken on added ideological importance because deskilling had undermined the ability of traditional craft workers to garner a strong sense of self-worth from their finely honed skills. For many unskilled male workers, masculine pride and self-worth also stemmed from the idea that they were tough enough to do hard work under difficult conditions. Hence the notion of women taking on certain jobs could be especially threatening.

Working men worried that a shift in the gender division of labour would undermine their privileged status. These worries were not unfounded. Although males continued to monopolize the best jobs in cotton mills, for example, some important changes took place. When cloth was made in the family household, women did the spinning. Under the factory system, however, men ran the new mule-spinning machine, which was large, heavy, complex, and was believed to require more physical strength than women could muster. A woman's skirt might also get caught in the machine's large moving carriage. But a newer, more productive ring-spinning machine required less skill and less physical strength and had no moving carriage. One of the main tasks of the ring spinner, piecing together broken ends of yarn, required nimble fingers. Spinning thus became women's work, and female ring spinners were replacing male mule spinners by the early twentieth century, at substantially lower rates of pay.

Meanwhile, the weaver's job had also changed. Under the old putting-out system (whereby entrepreneurs gave out the yarn to be woven at home), weaving had been mainly men's work. Under the factory system, however, the development of power looms and especially automatic looms in the late 1800s meant that many women became weavers. Automatic looms simplified the weaver's work considerably, thereby rendering this work more 'suitable' for women, and also making it possible to break the work down into a number of separate tasks to be performed by less-skilled and lower-paid employees, many of whom were women. In this case, technological change and an increased division of labour went hand in hand, increasing women's job opportunities, for a time.

Even though many jobs in the textile industry did not experience shifts in gender designation, there were some jobs that actually varied depending on the locale. In early-twentieth-century cotton mills, some jobs designated as predominantly male in parts of Quebec were performed chiefly by females in parts of the United States, and vice versa. These variations presumably reflected differences in local labour supplies, including ethnic variations.

The printing trade reveals how men could use their unions to exclude women from the better jobs. Traditionally, typesetting had been done by hand, demanded considerable skill, and was mainly a male job. The International Typographical Union largely succeeded in excluding women from typesetting. But the invention of the linotype machine towards the end of the nineteenth century threatened these male craft workers. Newspaper publishers argued that operating a linotype machine should be women's work since its keyboard resembled the typewriter, which was already identified with female labour. In Toronto, through a series of strikes, the male unionists succeeded in ensuring that men would be the ones who operated the new linotypes, at wage rates regulated by the union.

While women were kept out of 'men's jobs' in a variety of ways, married women in particular often faced special barriers to employment. Here, too, public pressure and co-workers' attitudes reinforced internalized norms and discriminatory employment policies. Many employers fired women workers when they married and refused to hire female employees who were already married. Women had often absorbed the idea that they should not be going out to work as wives, so in many cases they quit work upon marriage. Of course, the knowledge that employers would fire them when they married may have convinced women to leave work 'voluntarily.' Some desperately poor women hid their marriages so as to be able to retain employment. In firms that did employ married women, the wife who kept her job risked the disapproval of her co-workers and of society more broadly. This kind of disapproval was particularly intense during economic downturns, especially during the Great Depression, as we shall see. In addition, many husbands opposed their wives' employment outside their homes because it implied that the men were inadequate providers. Some husbands stopped their wives from going out to work even when the family badly needed the extra income.

Restricting women's access to paid employment was part and parcel of women's subordination in the family and in society more broadly. The logic of the family wage was faulty. While many people believed that women should not take 'men's jobs' because the men were their families' bread-winners, men who were not supporting families did not necessarily earn less than men who were. Nor did a man with five children to support earn more than a man with just one child. Moreover, the whole emphasis on the family wage was built on the presumption that the male head of the household would devote all his earnings to family needs. Although there were many 'good family men,' in other cases this was a doubtful proposition.

Ethnicity and Race

The gender division of labour intersected with ethnic and racist prejudices to exclude minority women from a wide range of 'women's jobs.' While employers had a great deal of power to determine whom to exclude from these jobs, the prejudices of other workers also often constrained minority women. Those affected included women from southern and eastern Europe, and especially those from China, Japan, and India. African-Canadian women – whose presence and disadvantaged position predated industrialization – and indigenous women also faced similar problems. At the same time, men's ability to monopolize many jobs was premised partly on the plentiful supply of low-wage male immigrants. Industrialists could keep labour costs down by hiring poorly paid male immigrants, rather than women, for many jobs where scarce skills were not required. During the second industrial revolution, in particular, employers in the manufacturing and resource sectors pressured immigration authorities to recruit men from southern and eastern Europe, as well as Asia. In periods of mass migration before the First World War and then again in the 1920s, sex ratios among immigrants were commonly skewed. Most male immigrants from southern and eastern Europe as well as Asia came alone as sojourners. The prospect of meagre earnings in Canada, customary restrictions against the long-distance migration of single women, and the family responsibilities of married women all contributed to keeping women close to home. In the case of the Chinese, the wife remained at home, not only to look after her husband's parents, but also to ensure that her sojourning husband would, in fact, return to China. In any case, women rarely had funds for travelling across the ocean.

Canadian policy makers saw Canada's need for heavy labour (e.g., in mining, railway construction, and steel plants) and assumed this was men's work. At the same time, employers in these sectors preferred a mobile labour force and hence frowned on male immigrants who were encumbered with families. By the turn of the century, Canada's immigration authorities were encouraging southern and eastern European families to settle on prairie farmland, but intense racism fuelled efforts to prevent Asian immigrants from becoming permanent settlers. Government officials made deliberate efforts to keep out Chinese women in particular. The head tax (entry tax) that each Chinese immigrant had to pay, beginning in 1885, was calculated not only to reduce the number of immigrant Chinese men but especially to reduce the number of women coming from China.

Those Chinese women who did come to this country could seldom obtain factory work, particularly in central Canada. Discrimination limited them to work for Chinese-Canadian employers in small restaurants, laundries, or fruit and vegetable businesses. Some Chinese-Canadian and Japanese-Canadian women found work in the fish canneries of British Columbia in the early twentieth century, sometimes working with babies strapped to their backs. But the main workforce in these plants consisted of Aboriginal women and immigrant Chinese men. Although Aboriginal females in northern canneries sometimes did jobs that were performed by immigrant Chinese males in less remote locations, Aboriginal women and Chinese-Canadian men did not do the same jobs in the same canneries. In this sector, the Aboriginal women received lower pay and even shorter stints of seasonal work than the immigrant Chinese males. Members of these groups obtained cannery jobs because the working season was too short and the pay was too low to attract males or females of European heritage.

Racist exclusion from other work and a perceived shortage of Euro-Canadian female workers led many Chinese males in western Canada to take conventionally female work. As Euro-Canadian miners struggled to push them out of the mines, Chinese immigrant men found jobs in British Columbia in domestic service, restaurants, laundries, and canneries. Some worked in shoe, cigar, and clothing factories at jobs typically filled by women in central Canada. These Chinese men were often stereotyped as effeminate. Racism was thus reinforced by linking Chinese males to the inferior status of women.

As they battled poverty, women and men of African descent also found that the intensity of racism barred them from many types of employment. Because men from this group earned such low wages, women's contributions to the family income were especially crucial. But African-Canadian women could generally work only as domestic servants. As one Toronto woman recalled, 'We weren't allowed to go into factory work until Hitler started the war.'

Among immigrants from southern and eastern Europe, women tended to marry relatively young, partly because of skewed sex ratios, and they tended not to go out to work. A significant number helped to build family farms out west or to run small family businesses in cities. Many who did work for wages were in domestic service or held related jobs as hotel maids or dishwashers and waitresses in restaurants. Some did typical 'women's jobs' in factories. Immigrant Ukrainian women, for example, worked in garment factories, cigar factories, paper-box factories, and meat-packing plants in cities such as Winnipeg, Montreal, and Edmonton. The clothing industry employed women from a number of backgrounds, including Italian, Polish, and Macedonian immigrants. Some women immigrants also found their way into southern Ontario's textile mills and canneries.

Immigrants frequently sought out workplaces where they could share the companionship and the familiar language of people from their own backgrounds. Jewish immigrants from eastern Europe exhibited one of the highest rates of occupational concentration. They gravitated towards the clothing industry not only because many other sectors would not hire Jews but also because of their cultural background and their experiences in eastern Europe. Many Jewish immigrants had worked in this sector before emigrating, partly because of severe anti-Semitic occupational restrictions and partly because of the religious injunction against wearing clothing that mixed wool and linen, which led religious Jews to depend on Jewish-made clothing to avoid violating sacred law. In Canada, the Jews already entrenched in the garment industry attracted many more, forming a concentration that helped maintain Jewish cultural practices and the Yiddish language. Yet, on the whole, economic factors and discriminatory employment practices probably played stronger roles than culture in determining the occupational distribution of particular racial and ethnic groups.

Service Jobs

Many females seeking work because of pressing economic need took jobs as domestic servants, especially if other jobs were not available to them. For a long period, this was the most common job for females, accounting for approximately one-third of all females who went out to work at the beginning of the twentieth century. Because industrialization and urbanization led more women to try for jobs in factories, offices, and shops, the relative importance of domestic service declined somewhat, to about one-fifth of the female workforce in the interwar years. Yet it remained an important occupation for females as middle-class housewives sought to employ a live-in domestic servant to lighten their own domestic work and to symbolize their family's status.

Most working-class women who went out to work preferred factory work to domestic service. Many of them felt that it was degrading to serve others in this way. Indeed, employers usually expected servants to be highly deferential. Although some employers were kinder than others, the 'mistress' commonly 'consider[ed] the servant a piece of machinery to perform her work,' according to a disheartened 'servant girl' who wrote a letter to the editor of the Toronto *Globe* in 1886. The live-in servant also suffered from lack of privacy and from isolation from family and friends. Her isolation was especially intense in situations where she was the only servant, as was commonly the case. Women who toiled in other people's homes frequently lost the possibility of having families of their own. The pay was low, the work was heavy: hauling water, scrubbing and polishing floors on their hands and knees, scouring pots and pans, and so on. The hours were unusually long. Many were on call twenty-four hours a day, perhaps with only a half day off per week. One woman explained her avoidance of such work: 'I don't like being bossed so much ... At the factory, when your work's done, your time's your own. You can go where you like.' In addition, the servant was sometimes subjected to sexual harassment by males in the household. If she fell out of favour and lost her job, she lost her bed and board as well. Hence many women who needed to earn a living avoided domestic service if they possibly could. The result was a great deal of transiency in this occupation and an overall shortage of servants.

A poignant letter from an early-twentieth-century servant to a Toronto newspaper portrayed some of the occupational difficulties. 'All day long I serve and scrub and bake and then wash dishes, polish silver, press clothes until well into the night,' the writer explained. 'I wear a frilly head band that seems like a lead weight on my throbbing temples ... I say "Yes sir," and "Yes madame" with a pleasant smile, when I feel like screaming and telling the whole shooting match to go to hades ... I am tender with [the employer's] little children and I humor their childish whims; my own are in a foster home and indifferently cared for. But I do it all gladly, and I am well satisfied that my meagre wage is enough to pay for the bite that keeps my children alive.'

The status of domestic service had declined since the early nineteenth century. In this earlier period, a farm family might have employed a domestic servant who was from a nearby farm. She may even have been a relative, and her family may have owned their own land, even if they were struggling to make ends meet. She was probably called a 'help' rather than a 'servant.' Although there were, of course, cases in this early period where the social distance between servant and mistress was greater than this, the distance between the two increased under the impact of urbanization and industrialization. The influx of Irish immigrant women into domestic service in the mid-nineteenth century, at a time when the Irish were often scorned, also contributed to the declining status of this occupation.

The overall shortage of servants led to late-nineteenth-century immigration schemes to bring over 'suitable' recruits from the British Isles, especially from England. The Canadian government, steamship companies, women's organizations in Britain and Canada (such as the YWCA and the National Council of Women of Canada), and the Salvation Army set up various schemes to guarantee employment, advance money for the Atlantic crossing, and escort groups of women to their new jobs. But some 'unsuitable' women took advantage of these schemes, and the shortage of domestic servants continued to be a problem.

A high proportion of immigrant domestic servants came from Britain, but some also came from continental Europe, particularly in the 1920s when fewer British women were available. In that decade, immigration restrictions on women from 'non-preferred' countries ensured that single women from central and eastern Europe could gain admission to Canada only if they promised to work as domestics. Even that door slammed shut with the intense immigration restrictions of the Great Depression. Meanwhile, overtly racist immigration policies also ensured that female domestic servants from Asia and the Caribbean were excluded from Canada until the 1950s.

Domestic service was the most common occupation for women from Finland, partly because their lack of familiarity with English prevented them from obtaining more desirable white-collar work and partly because many prospective employers no doubt liked their northern European origins and believed that Finnish women were especially clean and hard working. Although some domestic servants were day workers, living in provided certain benefits, especially for the newly arrived immigrant. She did not have to search for housing or spend money equipping her own home, and she could learn some Canadian customs. For immigrant and non-immigrant alike, domestic service usually meant a steady job without seasonal layoffs. Not all immigrants welcomed this work, however. Immigrant women from Hungary, for example, were averse to domestic service and to related jobs in the service sector. One such immigrant recalled that she often cried when she was forced to serve as a maid in a small hotel 'because at home we looked down on servants, and I kept thinking that I never had to work as a servant in Hungary and here in Canada I had to do it.' Even with no language barrier and often with Canadian-born status, African-Canadian women had no alternative. 'You couldn't get any position, regardless who you were and how educated you were, other than housework [as a domestic servant],' explained one woman who came to Toronto in 1920, 'because even if the employer would employ you, those that you had to work with would not work with you.'

In this context, some Anglo-Celtic domestic servants tried to assert their own dignity by differentiating themselves from those whom they considered more lowly. One woman who did housecleaning on a non-live-in basis, protested to her employer: 'Any lady I have been cleaning for always made my lunch and set it in a clean place. I am neither a pig nor a Chinaman. I am just as much a lady as you are ... [The other employers] all treat me like a human being, so here is your pail, you go get me my money and clean your dirty house yourself.'

Related jobs in the service sector included not only hotel maids but also laundry workers and restaurant staff. These were low-status jobs commonly requiring little training but much endurance. Laundry workers were on their feet all day, and their work was heavy, particularly in hand laundries. As a factory inspector reported at the turn of the century, they also had to cope with an 'atmosphere vitiated by gas and other impurities, which have continued to accumulate during the whole day, and the workers then inhale it at a time when the body is fatigued by a full day's work.' In addition to headaches and sore eyes from exposure to these fumes, they faced intense heat and other hazards. In restaurants, women worked as waitresses and as kitchen help and cooks. The pace could be frantic, especially during the lunchtime rush. As one early-twentieth-century waitress explained to a reporter, 'We have long hours, small pay and much abuse, not only from employers, but from many men who would not dare to treat their wife or sister as they do us.'

Prostitution

When women's job choices were so limited and the available jobs commonly entailed such harsh circumstances and low pay, some women turned to prostitution. While many commentators viewed prostitutes as depraved and sinful women and argued that it was their depravity that turned them into prostitutes, some working-class voices held that women turned to prostitution because otherwise they could not earn enough to eat. Although some, like Toronto's Mayor William Howland, believed that 'a good woman will die first,' others differed sharply. 'Is it any wonder that girls go wrong?' asked an 'Unemployed Working Girl' in a letter to one of the garment unions in 1914. Explaining that one Toronto clothing firm offered an experienced female worker a mere four dollars per week, she declared that such meagre wages could not be stretched to cover room and board and other absolute necessities. Some of those who turned to prostitution in desperation did so on a temporary basis, depending on the availability of other jobs, while others resorted to prostitution on the side to supplement their earnings from 'respectable' jobs that did not pay a living wage.

The circumstances of some live-in domestic servants drove them to prostitution. Some had been seduced or raped by male employers and then lost their jobs. Having been 'dishonoured' and kicked out on the streets, such women may have had little recourse other than prostitution, partly because they usually needed a letter of reference from the former employer (or other evidence of 'good character') in order to obtain a new position in domestic service. Besides, as 'fallen women,' they could not realistically expect that marriage would rescue them from the need to be self-supporting.

But while some desperate women resorted to prostitution as a survival strategy, others were tricked or trapped into this line of work. Horrified moral reformers publicized sensationalist stories of 'pure,' unsuspecting, young women caught in the grips of the 'white slave trade' and forced into a life of prostitution. According to these accounts, procurers lured women through false promises of marriage or even fake marriage ceremonies and sometimes drugged and kidnapped them. While such stories were exaggerated, some women were undoubtedly coerced into prostitution.

This was not the whole story, however, for some women workers apparently became prostitutes because they believed that work in the sex trade was easier and more lucrative than toiling away at a 'legitimate' job such as domestic service or garment work. They may have believed that prostitution would enable them to escape to a life that provided for more than bare necessities. Domestic servants who saw first-hand how the middle class lived, and department store employees who toiled in the midst of a multitude of appealing goods they could not afford on their meagre salaries, may have been especially susceptible to such dreams.

There was a hierarchy among prostitutes. Those who serviced wealthy customers might earn a great deal and work in luxurious surroundings, at least for a time, and a few might achieve upward mobility, becoming wealthy 'madams' who ran their own 'high-class' brothels. Raw frontier towns like Dawson City, in the Yukon, provided special possibilities because of their raucous atmosphere and high numbers of single men. Yet many prostitutes faced police harassment, imprisonment, fines, violence at the hands of pimps and customers, and intense social ostracism (including from their own families). They also risked sexually transmitted diseases such as syphilis and gonorrhea (especially before the development of penicillin in the 1940s), as well as unwanted pregnancies, sometimes leading to death from botched illegal abortions. The stress arising from the hazards of the job, together with the stigma of being social outcasts, led to high rates of alcoholism and drug addiction, especially to morphine and heroin, which resulted in further health problems.

Women from especially disadvantaged backgrounds may have felt driven to prostitution because discrimination sharply limited their prospects for employment and earnings in 'legitimate' sectors. The immigrants among them may have been especially vulnerable to procurers' machinations because they felt lost in a strange, new country. Among the worst off were Vancouver's immigrant Chinese 'crib prostitutes' at the turn of the century. Having been forced into prostitution under miserable working conditions in tiny cells, their impoverished 'careers' typically lasted only six to eight years before death. Moreover, prostitutes from 'non-preferred' immigrant groups, together with African-Canadian and First Nations prostitutes, faced especially harsh treatment from the legal system.

Conclusion

While prostitution constituted one of the most difficult options for women needing to earn money, most female job seekers encountered serious limitations in many other areas as well. Industrial capitalism had changed Canadian society fundamentally, transforming much of the world of work. Within the factories, women were commonly channeled into jobs perceived as resembling the kinds of unpaid work performed by housewives. The gender division of labour seemed natural, relegating women to jobs that required nimble fingers, patience, and attentiveness to detail – but not mechanical ability or the exercise of individual judgment. Yet many women preferred factory work to domestic service even though factory work commonly entailed harsh circumstances and low pay. Women from non-Anglo-Celtic backgrounds faced further obstacles that limited their employment options. In broad terms, some of the worst outrages of industrial capitalism pertained to women's work. In view of the particularly grim conditions women workers often experienced, it would prove difficult to reconcile the idealized image of women as fundamentally domestic beings with the reality of so many women going out to work.

2

White Collars

In 1919, Ellen M. Knox, principal of Havergal College (an exclusive private school for girls in Toronto), published *The Girl of the New Day*, a career advice book aimed at middle-class girls. Although she did not specify the social class of her intended audience, her references to them as cultured and educated make clear that she had in mind privileged young women. These girls, she claimed, were very fortunate because of the many honourable 'professions' open to them: teaching, nursing, social service, librarianship, office work, and 'salesmanship.' For her, these occupations were professions requiring education and training, and providing their practitioners with decent pay, social status, and opportunities for advancement, as well as the possibility of contributing to the public good. How accurate were Knox's views of these occupations and the opportunities they offered girls reaching adulthood in the late nineteenth and early twentieth centuries? Did their privileged class position permit middle-class girls to overcome the constraints gender ideology placed upon their working-class counterparts during the same period?

By the early twentieth century, the development of urban industrial society and the expansion of the public school system did open a range of white-collar occupations to women, providing higher status and better pay than manufacturing or domestic service. In 1901 almost one-quarter of all employed females held white-collar jobs, and by 1921 nearly one-half, a proportion that held for the next two decades. A few women – such as physicians Emily Stowe and Jennie Trout and lawyer Clara Brett Martin – succeeded in challenging male professional monopolies in high-status areas such as medicine, law, architecture, and engineering.

Teaching

Large numbers of women obtained teaching jobs as the public educational system expanded in mid-nineteenth-century British North America. Women were hired because they could be paid less than men. Many were hired first in impoverished areas, where school boards could not afford to pay the salaries of male teachers, and in resource areas where men were not interested in teaching, as more lucrative employment opportunities were available to them. Yet professional police forces, which were also developing at the same time as state-financed elementary school systems, did not hire women, despite the lower cost of their labour. Policing was considered a masculine occupation, whereas women were believed to have a special aptitude for teaching children, especially the very young. Accordingly, as larger schools emerged in urban areas, with pupils separated into different grades by age, women were hired for low wages to teach the lowest grades. Men monopolized better-paid and higher-status jobs in the school system such as principals, school inspectors, and superintendents.

Other cultural factors could also combine with gender ideology. In some parts of Nova Scotia, for example, the tradition of the Scottish parish school system militated against the hiring of women teachers because parish teachers traditionally performed certain religious functions that were not considered appropriate for women. In contrast, the work of nuns in Catholic teaching orders in Quebec, from the beginning of European settlement, may well have contributed to the acceptability of lay women teachers in that province.

Among French Canadians, certain groups of nuns specialized in developing a network of Catholic schools. Between
1841 and 1920, in particular, the Congregation of Notre
Dame established 151 convent schools. Nuns who were involved in education generally had more autonomy and
better opportunities for advancement than lay women teachers. It was not as difficult for nuns to become school principals or, in effect, school inspectors, and membership in the
Congregation of Notre Dame could improve a woman's
access to advanced training in the field of education.

The employment of female teachers could be controver-
sial. Like male craft workers, male teachers feared competition from women. By accepting low salaries, they argued,
women would degrade the profession and drive out qualified men. Male administrators also feared that women teachers would lower educational standards: they believed that
women were generally not capable of teaching the more
advanced pupils. Some critics believed that women were
intellectually inferior to men. Hence the Dundas County
superintendent wrote in 1858 that few women possessed the
'mental ability and decision of character' required for success in the schoolroom. Other critics argued that female
teachers could not attain the skills of male teachers because
of their brief stay within the profession.

The domestic ideology could be used to contain such
fears by rationalizing the confinement of women to the
lowest grades, with remuneration significantly less than that
of their male counterparts. Many educational reformers,
school administrators, politicians, and members of the general public believed that women had a natural aptitude for
teaching and a responsibility for the moral education of the
young. Thus they frequently did not acknowledge women's
teaching as an acquired skill, worthy of the same respect
and remuneration as the skills that male teachers necessarily acquired through higher education and experience. The
youth and supposed inexperience of most female teachers
also contributed to the undervaluation of their work. Their

low pay and their subordinate positions within the educational hierarchy were justified by the fact that so many of them retired from the profession when they married, 'just as their experience was beginning to make them really efficient.' Women also received lower pay than men because they were considered supplementary wage earners without dependants.

As was the case with factory workers, however, such arguments about women's transiency and skills owed far more to prevailing ideology than to reality. Girls started to teach as early as age fifteen; thus, they could easily have a decade or more of experience before marriage. Moreover, many men stayed in the profession just as briefly. While the undervaluation of women's work in teaching undoubtedly encouraged many to leave, even those inclined to stay on faced a bar against hiring married women. In the words of a nineteenth-century Nova Scotia school inspector, 'Married ladies are necessarily unable to give steady attendance to school duties, the higher law of maternity compelling them often to be at home ... The family is the school in which the married lady should teach.'

Teacher training and certification reinforced women's subordination. Qualifications to teach in British North American and, later, Canadian public schools were obtained either by certification examinations or by attendance at teacher-training schools. There were different classes of certificates, and only the highest ones qualified individuals to teach senior students and to obtain administrative positions. In Ontario, where the majority of teachers qualified through examinations, women were exempt from a number of areas in certification examinations that were required of men. Precisely because women had little chance of promotion, women teachers frequently aimed only for the lower-class certificates, which enabled them to begin teaching and earning faster. They believed that lengthier preparation for the first-class certificate was a waste of time. Women admitted to the Ontario Normal School, which trained the elite of the province's teachers, were accepted at a lower age than men, probably because maturity was less important since they would only assist men who were in charge of running the schools. In Nova Scotia, women teachers were ineligible to obtain the highest teaching licence, which would have permitted them to teach in high schools.

Some of the tasks that they were expected to perform and the degree of control exerted over their behaviour by school trustees bring into question the view of female teachers as independent professionals. During the early phases of the development of a state-financed public school system, in the early nineteenth century, both male and female teachers were believed to be no better than the 'lowest menials.' Women teachers were equated with 'spinsters and household servants,' and had such menial tasks as laying fires, cleaning schoolhouses, and shovelling snow. As late as 1923 the contract of a young teacher in Ontario spelled out her responsibility for keeping the schoolroom clean by scrubbing it with soap and water at least once a week. The contract also attempted to regulate the teacher's attire and conduct, both inside and outside the school. She was not to wear dresses in bright colours or with hems more than two inches above the ankle. She was not to use face powder and mascara or dye her hair. She was also forbidden to ride in a carriage or automobile with any man except her brothers or father. Nor was she to leave town without permission, loiter downtown in ice cream parlours, smoke cigarettes, or drink beer, wine, or whiskey.

Despite such restrictions, women of many social backgrounds wanted to become teachers. In a context of severely limited options, teaching was one of the few professions deemed appropriate for women, because, although they were working for pay outside the home, they were performing the supposedly maternal task of caring for children and transmitting moral values to them. Indeed, for those practitioners who were not driven to work by economic necessity, teaching could provide the satisfaction of carrying out a mission by transmitting the 'right values' to children of workers and immigrants, whom they viewed as social inferiors in need of uplifting. That is why some female university graduates entered teaching even when their qualifications exceeded those required by provincial authorities. Those of more modest background, who would depend upon their earnings, could qualify to teach quickly and thus start at a young age. Moreover, although poorly paid in comparison to their male counterparts, their average salaries in cities such as Toronto and Halifax compared very favourably with earning possibilities in other occupations open to women by the later half of the nineteenth century.

Taking jobs in remote frontier schools in northern Ontario, the prairie West, or British Columbia allowed some women to defy the constraints of the domestic ideology. Consider, for example, the case of a young convent-educated Ontario woman who accepted a position in Hope, British Columbia, in 1888, on the basis of a newspaper advertisement. She could travel by train only as far as Yale, BC. From there she travelled in a canoe, accompanied by two Native guides. Another teacher, on Vancouver Island in the early 1900s, rode sixteen kilometres a day on her bicycle to reach her school and also played the saxophone for the dances held in the local schoolhouse.

Teaching had become a highly feminized occupation by the turn of the century. Women teachers filled around four-fifths of the jobs during the first four decades of the twentieth century. The number of female teachers increased from approximately 31,000 in 1901 to some 50,000 in 1921 and roughly 65,000 in 1931 and 1941. These relatively large numbers reflected Canada's dramatic population growth and the further development of a school system that was free and compulsory.

Nursing

The tension between respectable femininity and paid employment emerged in nursing as well. At first glance nursing would appear to be perfectly acceptable for women, with its emphasis on nurturing, caring, and healing. The Methodist publication *Christian Guardian* described nursing as 'the employment for which the natural tenderness of women especially fits them.'

A nurse's work changed significantly after the 1870s, with the introduction of formal training. For much of the nineteenth century, the role of germs was not widely understood; consequently doctors had little to offer in terms of effective treatments and sometimes did considerable harm through traditional 'cures' and unsanitary conditions. Hospitals were commonly holding places for the poor and chronically ill, and many nurses were domestics or charwomen without formal training, whose duties consisted mainly of personal service tasks such as bedside care of patients and cleaning. In fact, old-style nurses had a reputation for drinking and roughness, although nursing nuns enjoyed higher status. After 1874, however, when the first hospital nursing school opened in Canada, nursing became one of the few skilled occupations with a formal apprenticeship process open to women. As a result, these trained practitioners obtained higher status and better wages than most other occupations open to women.

Yet even nursing could be viewed as disreputable. A young woman who embarked on this career in the early 1930s recalled: 'Father declared if I left to become a nurse, I need not return home.' With the deftness of the short-story writer, Alice Munro explains these concerns. When the protagonist in 'Love of a Good Woman,' Enid, has almost completed her nurse's training, her dying father begs her to promise that she will not become a nurse. Enid's mother tells the uncomprehending Enid that 'the part of nursing her father objected to was the familiarity nurses had with men's bodies. Her father thought – he had decided – that such familiarity would change a girl, and furthermore that it would change the way men thought about that girl. It would spoil her good chances and give her a lot of other chances that were not so good. Some men would lose interest and others would become interested in the wrong way.'

Early student nurses themselves recoiled from coming into contact with strange men's bodies. In a Halifax hospital, owing to a shortage of male attendants, the superintendent of nursing announced in 1896 that student nurses would have to bathe male patients and provide them with bedpans, catheters, suppositories, and enemas. Although the students did not openly protest against this new requirement, they were so averse to performing these duties that male patients complained of neglect. The hospital was forced to investigate and to continue to employ male orderlies to carry out duties deemed unsuitable for women.

Female nursing students were in great demand in the late nineteenth and early twentieth centuries, especially as hospitals became respectable therapeutic centres and more hospitals emerged in response to patient demand. Nurses in training, in particular, provided growing hospitals with a cheap labour force. During a three-year period the nursing students were housed and fed but received only a nominal stipend in exchange for carrying out many important duties: they prepared and administered medicine, kept records, cleaned and fed patients, and administered the daily operations of the wards. Their presence guaranteed the respectability of doctors' and hospitals' treatment of female patients. Hospitals could hire out student nurses for service in private homes under the guise of providing them with a variety of nursing experiences, meanwhile collecting and keeping their wages. By the 1920s there were about two hundred hospital schools in Canada; the apprenticeship system that they developed remained the dominant form of nurses' training until the 1940s. In many hospitals student nurses constituted almost the entire nursing staff. The overall number of nurses skyrocketed from only about 300 in 1901, to over 21,000 by 1921, and over 38,000 by 1941.

To overcome public suspicion, the respectability of nursing students had to be assured. Thus, only young women of good character, with a letter of reference from a clergyman, were admitted. Students were subjected to strict discipline. Their training was structured on a hierarchical family model: doctors and male administrators assumed the paternal role, while female nursing superintendents assumed the part of the wife who ensured the smooth functioning of patient care. The female students were cast in the role of dutiful daughters or female servants. At an Ontario hospital, nursing students were instructed to stand still if a doctor spoke and to rise and stand still when a graduate nurse came into the room. Nursing students were also expected to safeguard the reputation of their schools and hospitals by following strict guidelines of behaviour. They were forbidden to socialize with male staff or with patients. Nurses' uniforms, reminiscent both of nuns' habits and elite servants' uniforms, symbolized sexual neutrality and subordination. To safeguard their morality, the students were also expected to take part in religious observance.

Within a sex-segregated labour force, even graduate nurses could be paid relatively low wages. Their training ensured, moreover, that they would be 'appropriately' subordinate to male doctors and male hospital administrators. At the same time, they enjoyed advantages of status and pay relative to other staff members and to women workers in many other fields.

After graduation, most nurses in the early twentieth century became private-care nurses. Their work provided them with relative autonomy and a living wage that enabled them to live with their families, on their own, or in shared accommodation with their peers. Community and public-health nursing jobs were less numerous and more difficult to obtain. They required more training than private-duty and hospital nursing or work for private charitable agencies.

Recognizing the importance of public-health nursing during the influenza epidemic of 1918–19, the Canadian Red Cross began funding university-based courses in public-health nursing. Yet these workers received lower pay than their colleagues who worked for private agencies. Nevertheless, this type of nursing appealed to reform-minded women and even allowed some nurses to escape the constraints of docile, submissive femininity. Nurses who worked in schools and 'well-baby clinics' or who served as district and industrial nurses could bring their professional knowledge to help the poor and immigrants, especially the women and children in these groups. Public-health nursing in sparsely populated areas required an independent spirit and carried heavy responsibilities. Nurses in such areas travelled great distances to see their patients, sometimes on horseback or by sleigh, or by using hand-cars on railway tracks. In the absence of doctors, they frequently took full charge of patient care.

Social Work

A younger profession than teaching and nursing, social work grew out of the rapid industrialization and urbanization of turn-of-the-century Canada. The existing charitable organizations were too small to deal efficiently with all the new social and economic problems. Many such organizations in Canada's larger cities were therefore centralized under a paid welfare bureaucracy. In the 1920s, municipal, provincial, and federal governments assumed more and more responsibility for public welfare, in such areas as relief, mothers' allowances, minimum-wage boards, and child welfare. Both private and public welfare bureaucracies were staffed increasingly by female university graduates, who became the majority of front-line workers. As 'caseworkers,' they were deployed to investigate or diagnose the problems of people who sought social assistance and, on the basis of these investigations, to offer a 'cure' for their problems.

More than in other white-collar occupations, the women themselves used the domestic ideology actively and deliberately to legitimate the female presence in social work. Middle- and upper-class female volunteers in reform associations had prepared the way for paid female social workers by invoking gender ideology about women's maternal responsibility to justify venturing beyond the domestic sphere to look after others. Increasingly, social service came to be seen as a woman's field. At the same time, many young women who came to work in settlement houses, private charities, and welfare institutions were motivated by more than the desire for social reform. They were seeking new, paid jobs suitable for female university graduates.

The maternalist ideology that helped open new opportunities for women also handicapped those who worked to transform social work into a paid profession. As in nursing and teaching, economic reasons were central to the feminization of this profession. Maternalist arguments served to keep both the salaries and the status of women social workers low. The tendency to ascribe women's success in social work to their womanly intuition or their motherly character undervalued their education, training, and experience, all of which might otherwise have justified higher pay. Indeed, the newness of the field cast doubts on claims to special skills and qualifications. While some 'feminine' attributes supposedly made women excellent case workers, other such attributes apparently prevented them from rising to the highest ranks of the profession. Women were seen as too emotional and too soft to carry out administrative and executive tasks, especially those related to handling public money. During the Depression, for example, female social workers employed by Ottawa's Public Welfare Board were blamed for rising relief costs. As a result, the women were fired from their positions and replaced by male detectives. Low pay and low status were also justified on the grounds that most social workers were single. They were believed to have no dependants, and were expected to retire from the field once they married.

By the 1930s, a number of women in social work who were concerned to enhance its professional status began to argue that this would be possible only if more trained males became social workers. Charlotte Whitton, one of the leading female social workers, took feminist positions on many issues, and yet even she argued, '"Lord give us men." Speaking absolutely professionally, there are administrative problems which are by their weight beyond the nervous capacity of the average woman to carry for a long time.'

Clerical Work

Until the late nineteenth century, men did all clerical work. As women entered this area, a dramatic transformation took shape. In the first half of the twentieth century, the number of female clerical workers increased astronomically, from under 9,000 in 1901 to almost 79,000 in 1921 and over 152,000 in 1941. Meanwhile, the proportion of clerical workers who were female rose from under a quarter in 1901 to half by 1941. Moreover, clerical workers accounted for a higher and higher proportion of all female participants in the paid labour force, rising from under 4 per cent in 1901 to almost 19 per cent in 1941.

In the small nineteenth-century offices of banks, insurance companies, and factories, young men had been hired to perform all manner of office work. They needed familiarity with the functioning of the office so that they could rise to higher positions. But such an approach was no longer efficient by the turn of the century, as the great expansion of manufacturing, financial, and commercial establishments in Canada, and the growth of the public service bureaucracy, increased the volume of office work. Growing labour needs provided the incentive to hire women workers. As in factory administration, office managers found that by dividing work into simple, repetitive tasks they could cheapen labour and control it more effectively. Using the prevailing assumptions about masculine and feminine natures, they assigned the new types of office work to women. They believed that, while men would be unfit and unwilling to undertake this type of work, women were ideally suited to perform it. According to a leading early-twentieth-century advocate of 'scientific' office management, 'a woman is preferred for the secretarial position, for she is not averse to doing minor tasks, work involving the handling of petty details, which would irk and irritate ambitious young men.'

These assumptions meant that the incoming female clerks did not generally displace men, who continued to be hired as accountants and bookkeepers and for other jobs with prospects for advancement. Women took the new, routinized jobs. The monotonous, dead-end character of the work meant that they could be poorly paid. This combination of gender stereotyping and economic advantages for the employer helps explain why the introduction of new, gender-neutral technology, such as the typewriter and other business machines, hastened the feminization of the office. Because the operation of the typewriter required training but held out no promise of advancement or economic advantage, men were not drawn to it. Educated women, however, whose employment prospects were severely limited by gender ideology, saw greater promise in jobs created by the new machine. After all, typewriting and stenography, which were linked together until the First World War, required some skill and a higher level of literacy than factory or sales work, and office workers generally benefited from a cleaner and safer working environment. Although typists and stenographers earned considerably less than male clerks, their salaries nevertheless exceeded the average wages of women workers. In addition, the men with whom these women worked – or, more likely, under whom they worked – were generally of higher social standing than factory operatives and were therefore believed to be more respectable. Consequently, as the use of the typewriter spread, by the turn of the twentieth century most typists were women.

Special business schools emerged to train women, particularly in shorthand and typing. The notion of being a 'business girl' had prestige, even though it seldom meant that a young woman was in business for herself. Nor did it mean that she was able to obtain a significant managerial position in the business world. The ranks of these business schools nevertheless increased and even included female university graduates, whose qualifications far exceeded job requirements. Moreover, in the mid-1920s, the University of Western Ontario introduced a degree course in secretarial science. The domestic ideology helped explain away the discrepancy between women's lowly status as female clerks and their superior education: even if their education were not fully utilized on the job, it would contribute to making them good mothers once they retired from the paid workforce.

Following the First World War, managers found that the ready supply of female labour allowed them to alter women's office work still further. Stenographers' work was subdivided. Early on, stenographers required knowledge of shorthand in order to take personal dictation. They worked in different departments and performed a variety of tasks. But the introduction of dictation machines, or dictaphones, brought in a new category of workers – the typists who no longer required shorthand but simply transcribed material directly from the dictaphones and performed other routine jobs such as updating mailing lists or typing forms. Their status and pay were thus lower than those of stenographers. Their working conditions were also poorer. Working exclusively on the typewriter strained hand joints, muscles, backs, and shoulders. Most regimented was the work of women concentrated in one area of the office: the typing pool. The pool supervisor had control over the pace and flow of work, assigning work and keeping a close eye on the punctuality, productivity, and accuracy of each typist. Once typewriting came to be defined as women's work, the operation of other business machines such as adding machines and calculators followed suit.

The feminization of office work did not occur simultaneously in all sectors. In banking, for example, women's entry as tellers lagged behind their employment as general clerks and stenographers. Tellers dealt with the public, and it was widely believed that only men could elicit the public trust necessary for successful banking operations. In this case, class prejudices were stronger than gender bias. When the First World War created a shortage of socially respectable, middle-class men, bankers believed that women of the same class background would enjoy greater public confidence than educated working-class men.

Developments in the civil service took shape somewhat differently. When merit, determined by entrance examinations, replaced patronage as the basis for appointments in 1908, women flooded into the civil service. As in teaching, the influx of women aroused fears that the status of the occupation would decline and thus disrupt (male) recruitment into the higher levels of the civil service. In 1918, the Civil Service Commission therefore began classifying job openings by sex. In 1921, married women were barred from holding permanent posts in the civil service (with only a few exceptions). These new regulations restricted women to the lowest ranks of the civil service. Not surprisingly, most women did not stay in these jobs for more than a few years, and the number of female civil servants actually declined between 1921 and 1931.

Sales Work

Sales clerks are sometimes classified as a subcategory of clerical workers. Yet neither popular views nor scholars agree about the status of this occupation, which began to open up for women decades before office work. According to some turn-of-the-century analysts and subsequent historians, work in sales was preferable to domestic and blue-collar work. Shopgirls not only worked in clean, attractive surroundings, but their attire, grooming, and familiarity with various consumer goods made them symbols of fashion. Their wages, though lower than those of their male counterparts, were nevertheless higher than the wages earned by most blue-collar women workers. Other studies emphasize that sales work required few skills and that even female clerks themselves recognized that there were no prospects for advancement. Some of them even took blue-collar jobs in the mail-order room of department stores, where they could make better wages. Others, according to a former Eaton's clerk, 'used to marry fellows they didn't even care for, to be free of Eaton's.'

The demand for sales clerks expanded between the 1880s and the 1930s as department stores, self-service grocery chains (such as Loblaws, Dominion, and Safeway), and drugstore chains cornered an ever-growing share of retailing in Canada. The number of female sales clerks increased dramatically in the early twentieth century, from 2,700 in 1901 to over 36,000 in 1921 and over 68,000 in 1941, while their proportion also rose dramatically, from about 15 per cent in 1901 to over 26 per cent in 1921 and some 41 per cent in 1941.

In a familiar fashion, retail labour became segmented along gender lines. In the larger establishments, management was separated from sales and rarely included women. In 1914 in Winnipeg department stores, for example, there was not one female department head among the 3,200 women employed in peak season. The highest position to which women could generally rise was that of assistant buyer. 'Women's nature,' particularly their supposed lack of independence of thought, was the main rationale for their restricted opportunities. According to a trade journal, women were suited for those branches of trade where 'dress and pleasant manners are really more necessary than mental ability.' Only in areas of supposed 'female expertise,' such as millinery (women's hats) and notions (small items for women such as ribbons and hair pins), did women sometimes attain management positions. Segmentation occurred at lower levels as well. In sales, women were restricted to the sale of lighter goods such as gloves, hosiery, laces, buttons, and ribbons, while male clerks sold heavier and more expensive goods such as carpets and home furnishings. To date the economic implications of this division have not been explored for the period before the Second World War. Research on the postwar period, however, makes clear that sales commissions in 'male' departments were much higher than in areas where women dominated. Women also worked as wrappers and cashiers. As Timothy Eaton told the Royal Commission on the Relations of Labour and Capital in Canada in 1888, he paid the average salesman twelve dollars but first-class saleswomen only six to eight dollars because 'girls are more apt when young ... But boys in time exert themselves more and aim at being something and to rise higher.'

The discipline that store managers and department superintendents imposed on their employees resembled that in factories. In some stores, clerks who arrived a few minutes late in the morning or returned a bit late after lunch were sent home for half a day without pay. Hours could be longer than in factories, and evening work for women was more common. Sales clerks faced the additional difficulty of having to stand for long hours. Cashiers were able to leave their stations only when store managers activated elaborate procedures to replace them, even if they simply needed to go to the washroom. Since they worked with the public, retail clerks were expected to dress well, despite their low wages. Contact with the public affected women differently from men in another way as well. The need for female clerks to serve strange men allowed for the possibility of improper advances and cast suspicions on their moral purity. Handling finery that they could not afford on their low wages was also thought to make them particularly vulnerable to seduction through gifts. Consequently, stores had strict regulations against interaction with men who came in 'just to talk with the girls.'

Feminine Respectability, Status, and Racist Exclusivity

Sales work resembled many other white-collar female jobs in its racist exclusivity. Apart from family-owned small businesses, stores generally did not employ minority women. Eaton's department store in Winnipeg (the city with the largest proportion of non-Anglo-Celtic immigrants prior to the Second World War) employed Jewish women only behind the scenes in the mail-order department. Minority women who were not 'visibly' different from the dominant Anglo-Celtic and French groups might get sales work by hiding their identities, especially by changing their names. One Jewish woman who disguised her origins to work at Eaton's lost her job when she stayed away from work on a Jewish holy day. A Chinese-Canadian woman recalled that, in British Columbia, she and other women from the same background 'would never go and apply for a job at Woodward's [department store]. They wouldn't even look at you.'

Office work was equally beyond the reach of minority women. For example, in Welland, Ontario, another community with a high proportion of non-Anglo-Celtic inhabitants, they were excluded until after the Second World War. According to a female Hungarian immigrant, 'they wouldn't even talk to you if your name was not English.' Another woman remembers that when she was in high school, African-Canadian girls who wanted to take commercial or secretarial courses were told, 'Well, who would want to hire you?'

Keeping minority women out of white-collar work reflects the striving to assert and maintain the status of these occupations. Prior to the Second World War the definition of feminine respectability in Canada was intimately linked to membership in Canada's two 'founding' nations: English Canadians and French Canadians. In a society that believed in a racial hierarchy, the association of any occupation with a minority group that was seen as inferior would inevitably lower the status of that occupation. Such exclusivity also served to reduce competition.

In teaching, social work, and nursing, the exclusion of minority women was more directly linked to the domestic ideology. Women in these occupations were supposed to be carrying out their maternal role of transmitting proper 'Anglo-Saxon,' 'Christian,' or 'Canadian' values to the young, the 'foreigners,' or the poor, who had supposedly not had the advantages of proper moral guidance. Such an important task could not be entrusted to women who were not part of the dominant groups. That is why in Ontario, for example, women of Jewish and eastern European origin, even if they were university graduates, were unable to get jobs in public schools. Similarly, prospective nurses from allegedly inferior groups were usually not accepted into training programs.

Such exclusionary practices, which lasted until after the Second World War, came into the open only when challenged. For example, when a Toronto resident and high-school graduate applied for admission to the nurses' training program at the Toronto General Hospital in 1940, she indicated in her letter that she was 'coloured.' She was told that there were no vacancies in the school. Well aware of racist prejudice in Toronto, she reapplied using a fictitious name and another address and without indicating her skin colour. This time she was invited for an interview. Having brought to light the existence of racist discrimination, she herself gave up, but her father pursued the matter through the Toronto Colored Liberal Association. The failure of his efforts to gain admission for his daughter illustrates that nurses themselves used their hard-won ability to regulate their profession to maintain racist exclusivity. The registrar of the Registered Nurses' Association of Ontario hid behind public disapprobation as a way of justifying the practice of denying training to minority women. She was certain that many patients and doctors would protest the introduction of 'coloured' nurses to the wards. Ontario's deputy minister of health conveniently pointed out that the provincial Nurses Registration Act did not allow for government intervention into the admissions policies of nursing schools.

Ironically, intense discrimination could create small niches for minority women in nursing and teaching. Thus Chinese- and Japanese-Canadian women were admitted to the nurses' training program at the Vancouver General Hospital in the 1930s, on the assumption that their own communities needed them. Having had the 'privilege' of being introduced to the values and morals of Canadian society through their professional training, these nurses could then help to lift members of their own groups out of 'the characteristics of the Dark Ages' in which they were still allegedly steeped.

Within the school system, the segregation of African-Canadian pupils in Ontario and Nova Scotia meant that African Canadians could find work as teachers. Indeed the racist climate meant that for most African-Canadian women, teaching was the only alternative to working as domestics. Since funding for such schools depended in part on taxes from impoverished African-Canadian communities, however, both the salaries and the working environments of these teachers lagged behind those of other teachers. But the sense that they were helping advance their people could serve to counterbalance African-Canadian teachers' poor pay and working conditions. A few women of non-Anglo-Celtic immigrant background found similar niches in the impoverished, bloc settlements on the Prairies, where inferior accommodation, low salaries, and cultural isolation made employment unappealing for Anglo-Canadian teachers. Indeed, as long as bilingual schooling was an option, immigrant school trustees showed a preference for teachers from their own ethnic backgrounds, whether male or female. Because of the concern about assimilation, however, the public school bureaucracy saw these teachers as less desirable than Anglo-Canadian teachers.

Conclusion

The rosy picture of career opportunities that Ellen Knox painted in *The Girl of the New Day* clearly exaggerated the employment prospects of the more privileged young women in Canada. Those who achieved quasi-professional status, in areas such as teaching and social work, found that they were treated as second-class members of their fields. Those who could not afford the training to enter the 'female professions' found that office and sales work had many disadvantages as well. Ellen Knox could be unconcerned about these constraints because she accepted the subordinate role for all women. That is why she discussed opportunities open to them in nursing but not medicine, in teaching but not law. The pinnacle of success for the female office worker was to become private secretary to her manager or, better still, assistant to the manager. Besides, Knox believed that for young women, 'the most honourable profession of them all was motherhood.' Meanwhile, she did not even consider how ethnic and racist prejudices constrained minority women. Her book was meant to advise white, Christian girls.

3

In Times of Crisis

The fate of employed women during the First World War (1914–18) and the Great Depression (1929–39), two crises that shook Canadian society in rapid succession, demonstrates the resilience of the gendered structure of the paid workforce. These crises exerted seemingly contradictory pressures on women workers but ultimately did not greatly alter their situation. During the war, the expansion of production, war casualties, and the enlistment of many men in the armed forces combined to create labour shortages that led to an increased demand for women workers. Although some women were recruited into jobs that had formerly been closed to them, many were urged to return to the domestic sphere at the war's end, to free up jobs for returning veterans. During the Great Depression, by contrast, amid unprecedented shrinkage in employment, many Canadians demanded that women withdraw from paid employment to free up jobs for unemployed men. Despite these pressures, there was no mass exodus of women from the paid labour force in the 1930s.

The First World War

During the First World War, one of the most dramatic and unconventional uses of female labour occurred in the munitions plants, a workplace previously deemed totally unsuited to women's nature. In fact, the munitions industry offers the best-documented case of women's wartime work in heavy industry. Despite their hesitancy to recruit women workers for the war effort, government officials reluctantly concluded, during the final years of the war, that women were badly needed. Officers of the Imperial Munitions Board (IMB) then pushed industrialists to hire women. Many of these employers disliked the plan, believing that factories would have to be retooled to adapt them to women's labour and that war contracts were too uncertain for such investments. Some employers hired women on a temporary basis until a specific contract was completed. Others took advantage of the war conditions not only to pressure all their workers to produce more, but also to accelerate breaking down jobs into simplified parts. They believed women could be used in the newly deskilled jobs. The fact that women could be utilized as low-wage labour made their employment more attractive to employers, for government officials failed to establish a firm equal-pay policy in the munitions industry.

At the height of munitions production, there may have been 35,000 female munitions workers in Ontario and Quebec (where this industry was concentrated), and they mainly made fuses and shells for the battlefields. While this constituted a major foray into non-traditional areas of work for women, they did not necessarily directly replace men, but tended to work at newly simplified tasks. In addition, the proportion of women was generally higher in the munitions plants that were newly built during the war, as opposed to pre-existing plants that were converted to the wartime manufacture of munitions. Clearly, the majority of munitions workers were still men. The main IMB official pushing employers to hire women apparently still thought that women lacked the strength and skill for certain munitions jobs. Women, moreover, continued to be placed in subordinate positions. 'Women under the guidance of trained toolmakers,' stated one IMB report, 'are efficient and useful.' Only notions of women's patriotic duty overrode concerns about their alleged frailty – at least temporarily.

Many women wanted this kind of work because it usually paid better than traditional women's jobs. At least some of the young women used their higher earnings to purchase fancy new clothes and proudly wore them to work. To the middle-class observer such behaviour simply illustrated the irresponsibility and frivolity of 'working girls' who 'spent money like water.' For these young women, however, dressing up was an assertion of their dignity and self-worth, signifying that they were just as good as wealthier women. It was also a way of brightening up lives that might otherwise have felt quite dreary.

Munitions work could be dangerous. As the representative of a deputation of female workers informed the *Toronto Star* in 1917: 'They are killing us off as fast as they are killing the men in the trenches.' She was complaining about the move to increase the women's already exhaustingly long working hours. Another woman who worked in one of these factories during the war recalled that 'Work there was a real endurance test. The factory was a hell hole, avenues of clanking, grinding, clashing machines with too much noise to talk ... and your feet wet all the time. It was dangerous; there were no covers for many machines, and you were splashed with chemicals. And my factory had a blasting furnace and no fire escape.'

There were sometimes compensations, however. One former munitions worker remembered the companionship she experienced on the job. Speaking of her female co-workers, she declared: 'They were a wonderful bunch, and I see so many of them to this day. It enriched my life really.' She herself was from a middle-class background and re-called that she learned a great deal about others: 'In meeting these people that we had never had any opportunity to meet before, and finding they were just the same as we were, but they just hadn't had the chances that we'd had for

education and that kind of thing, we began to realize that
we were all sisters under the skins.'

Women probably did not move into the paid labour force
to the extent that historians have commonly assumed. The
number of female workers in manufacturing increased from
70,700 in 1915 to a high of almost 113,000 in 1918. But the
number of male workers in factories increased at a roughly
similar rate. While 17.9 per cent of factory workers were
female in 1915, this figure had increased only to 18.7 per
cent by 1918. Moreover, the increase included women who
headed to traditionally female jobs in textiles and clothing
in response to the demand for military uniforms and other
war-related orders. Still, the tensions of this period cannot
be analysed simply in terms of numbers. The appearance of
just a handful of women in a non-traditional area could be
quite unsettling.

The war affected many white-collar jobs as well. By 1916,
women were being brought into traditionally male jobs in
stores, offices, and banks. In urban areas especially, bank
managers started using female tellers during the war despite their earlier conviction that only male tellers could
inspire public confidence. Interestingly, they were not paid
less than male clerks. Yet on average the salaries of female
bank employees would remain lower than those of male
employees because women had far fewer opportunities for
advancement. Concerns about the morality of female clerks,
together with the expectation that most would marry, led
employers to believe that women were not suited for careers in banks. Above all, female employees could not be
transferred from branch to branch, in the required pattern
for advancement, as it would be impossible to safeguard
their moral purity by providing appropriate lodging. More
broadly, the wartime shortage of male office clerks occurred
in the midst of the long-term restructuring of office work,
thereby accelerating the movement of women into office
jobs, many of which were newly routinized. Some women
lost their new office jobs at the war's end, but many did not.

As before the war, patterns of women's employment followed ethnic lines. Anglo-Celtic women in urban areas of central Canada got most of the new jobs in munitions factories and offices. The lower military enlistment rates in Quebec meant that there were fewer job openings for French-Canadian women. Women from certain minority groups were not trusted with war production, and instead took over the lower-status, poorly paid jobs that Anglo-Celtic women abandoned, especially in domestic service. In the depression just before the war, even these jobs had been closed to them.

There were serious fears that wartime disruptions in gender norms might turn out not to be temporary. Returning soldiers might find women entrenched in jobs that had belonged to the veterans. The placement of women workers in 'men's jobs' in areas not connected with war production intensified such concerns. The supposedly natural order of things was being violated. Higher wages might encourage women to become too independent and therefore reluctant to marry and have families, thus undermining postwar reconstruction. Consequently, women faced considerable public pressure to vacate traditionally male jobs at the war's end. 'Do you feel justified in holding a job,' one government propaganda bulletin asked, 'which could be filled by a man who has not only himself to support, but a wife and family as well?' Some of the pressure was far less subtle: certain employers simply fired women and replaced them with veterans. In any case, the munitions industry contracted sharply as the war ended, and both women and men lost their jobs. Overall, at least in factory work, women generally did not remain in non-traditional areas after the war. With the end of the wartime emergency, the rationale for their employment – and the jobs – vanished.

By the 1920s, however, the employment of young, single women had become more acceptable – as long as they were confined to low-wage 'women's work.' Paid work, as an interval between leaving school and marrying, had become more legitimate for females. This limited acceptance was premised on women's inferiority in the paid labour force. Canadians were becoming reconciled to the idea that such work would not be a grave threat to women's natures because these women would return to their true domestic calling upon marriage.

The Great Depression

In the depths of the Depression of the 1930s, a desperate woman who had worked as a bookkeeper and stenographer wrote to Prime Minister R.B. Bennett. When her employer went out of business, she could not find another job because so many others were looking for work as well. Her father, a poverty-stricken Manitoba farmer, could not help support her. She explained that, as she ran out of savings, 'my clothing became very shabby ... Many prospective employers just glanced at my attire and shook their heads.' 'First I ate three very light meals a day,' she continued. 'Then two and then one. During the past two weeks I have eaten only toast and drunk a cup of tea every other day. In the past fortnight I have lost twenty pounds and the result of this deprivation is that I am so very nervous that I could never stand a [typing] test along with one, two and three hundred girls.' Declaring that she would drown herself rather than resort to prostitution, she implored the prime minister to find her a job anywhere in Canada.

The Great Depression brought massive impoverishment. At its depths in 1933, the unemployment rate skyrocketed to over 25 per cent, a dramatic increase from the unemployment rate of slightly over 4 per cent four years earlier. Some estimates suggest that the unemployment rate reached 33 per cent that year. By early spring of 1933, over 1,400,000 urban dwellers were relying on relief to stave off starvation, as were several hundred thousand rural people, despite the fact that relief was hard to obtain and deliberately degrading.

As unemployment tore apart the social fabric, the fears associated with women entering the paid labour force intensified. Many people resented women who held jobs, and many Anglo-Celtic Canadians resented 'foreigners' who were allegedly taking good jobs or unfairly receiving relief payments. An unemployed veteran wrote to Prime Minister Bennett in 1934, criticizing him for failing to solve the Depression by reserving jobs for males. This writer maintained that men who had fought for Canada 'walk and walk and ask for work but none to be had while the women who powder their noses and waste their time talking nonsense take our jobs.' 'After all,' he continued, 'the men can and will be and are the Breadwinners[;] where there are girls working as well as other members of the family its [sic] too much[;] it should be stopped[;] they always spend their money on shows etc. besides having some Sugar Daddy take them out[;] its [sic] not fair.' He felt so desperate that he even threatened that if nothing were done about this problem, there would be a revolution.

Many believed that young, single women should be supported by their fathers rather than taking up scarce jobs. But the resentment was directed especially against married women who went out to work, for many people believed that the women's husbands could – and should – be supporting the family. Even single women workers claimed married women were just working for 'pin money' and should quit and depend on their husbands so that the allegedly more needy single women could have their jobs. Many Canadians argued that women should leave paid labour altogether. As the unemployed veteran's letter suggests, some argued that the whole economic crisis could be solved if all employed women left their jobs. In some of these scenarios, the newly employed men were then expected to marry and support the women.

It was not just the odd crank who maintained that women should 'return to the kitchen.' In 1933, Médéric Martin, former mayor of Montreal and a member of the Quebec

Legislative Assembly, publicly called on the federal government to pass legislation requiring each woman worker to give up her job to a male relative. In the meantime, Martin appealed to women's patriotism and altruism in asking them to quit voluntarily. Several such bills were promoted in Quebec's Legislative Assembly, although none passed. The most sweeping bill would have expelled every woman from the paid labour force unless she could demonstrate family need. Despite widespread hostility to female workers, the legislative approach was seldom pursued, partly because many public officials believed that employers had every right to hire whomever they wished, without state interference. At the same time, appeals continued to be made to employers to fire married women voluntarily.

The fear of gender role reversal gripped Canadians. The MP for Hull expressed this deepening anxiety as follows: 'We must correct a completely abnormal situation: one sees girls and even their mothers leaving the house to work, while the husbands and the male youths stay at home, looking after the children, and even doing the cooking.' Although recent research suggests that unemployed family men may have avoided minding the children and doing the housework, the 'threat' of the female breadwinner loomed large. Masculinity itself seemed under siege when men could not support their families. A woman who worked in Edmonton's relief office during the Depression stressed how upset were the men who were lining up for 'the dole': 'I've seen tears in men's eyes, as though they were signing away their manhood, their right to be a husband and sit at the head of the table and carve the roast.'

Some voices spoke up in defence of the working women. Most argued that their families desperately needed their earnings, especially where fathers and husbands were unemployed, underemployed, reeling from repeated wage cuts, or entirely absent. A few bold feminists argued that women had just as much right to work as men, regardless of economic need, but this argument was rare during the depression decade. More often, the right to work was combined with arguments about economic need. The most consistent advocates of women's right to work were members of the Canadian Federation of Business and Professional Women's Clubs, an organization composed of professionals, owners of small businesses, and office clerks. The federation passed a resolution in 1931 that condemned workplace discrimination based on women's marital status. Although most federation members were single, they believed that attempts to exclude married women were 'the thin edge of the wedge to get women out of positions in the professional and business world.' They also spoke out against the practice of lowering women's salaries, insisting that women's gains in the paid labour force were theirs 'by right of a difficult conquest and painstaking labor.' Yet by the late 1930s even the federation's president used the language of need rather than rights to justify her organization's defence of employed women. In a similar vein, most spokespersons for the National Council of Women of Canada (an umbrella organization for various women's groups) steered clear of the language of rights and argued that only financial need could justify married women's work. Only a few feminists, such as Judge Helen Gregory MacGill, noted that exclusion was not a solution to male unemployment because most men would not do 'women's jobs' anyway.

In fact, women did not withdraw from the paid labour force in large numbers. Like men, many women could not find jobs in the midst of such economic devastation. There were certainly some cases where women were fired and replaced with men, as in Quebec's textile industry. Such strategies were most commonly used in banks. As the western superintendent of the Imperial Bank of Canada told a female clerk when he fired her: 'The development of ... young men [in junior positions] has been retarded by the fact that ladies are occupying the positions that should be filled by young men.' In addition, some employers reacted to minimum wage laws for females by replacing women with lower-paid males, though poor enforcement of these laws meant that they probably had little impact on women's employment.

In fact, such substitution was limited. In a number of employment areas, female workers were apparently protected, to a significant degree, by their confinement to female jobs ghettos such as domestic service and stenography, where men would not work. In addition, women seem to have experienced somewhat lower unemployment rates than men. They were less vulnerable because they tended to work in – or shift into – areas of the economy not as hard hit as key areas of male employment such as fishing, logging, mining, and the construction industry. The service and clerical sectors in particular experienced significantly lower rates of unemployment, and these were sectors with high proportions of women.

Employers were in a strong position to dictate working conditions. Consequently, workers with jobs often experienced repeated wage cuts and an intensified pace of work. The clothing industry's notoriously poor conditions and low wages got worse, as special investigators discovered. Declining purchasing power reduced the demand for new clothing dramatically. The industry's peak seasons became shorter and shorter, and the hours during those periods were so long that sometimes workers would sleep in the plants instead of going home at night. An immigrant Jewish woman who worked in the dress trade in this period recollected having to work from eight in the morning to midnight for several weeks during the seasonal peak. Despite her efforts, her employer went bankrupt, and she was never paid for any of this work. Intense speed-ups brought so much strain and fatigue that, according to an investigator for the Royal Commission on Price Spreads, 'many of the girls said they were afraid they were going out of their minds.' One told the commission that the speed-ups left her so tired 'I could not eat my supper ... Going home on the street car, I would just dread getting a seat, because if I sat down, I could not get up again, my knees and my legs would be so stiff.' Another lost two months' work on account of 'nervous exhaustion.' The royal commission concluded in 1935 that these wages and working conditions 'merit the most emphatic condemnation.'

Many women coped with unemployment by looking for work as domestic servants. More married women found such work, and more Anglo-Celtic Canadians. Nonetheless, domestic service remained the chief occupation of women from central and eastern Europe and women of African descent. Families that continued to have a steady income through the 1930s found it easier to hire domestics because of the general decline in prices and wages. Some unscrupulous employers took advantage of women's desperation and hired them for extraordinarily little. Some even substituted used clothing or leftover food as part of their pay.

Yet, there were limits to how many unemployed women this sector could absorb, and some middle-class social reformers grew concerned about the single women who still could not find jobs. Legislators did little to help them, however. Indeed, the lawmakers denied that single women's unemployment constituted a serious problem, even though many more young women would have been out working during more normal times. Even the limited efforts to create work and hostels for single, unemployed men did not extend to their female counterparts. And even where single women did qualify for direct relief, the amount – which was not generous for any category of recipients – was especially inadequate for them. Agnes Macphail, the lone woman member of the House of Commons, was struck by the hypocrisy: 'A great deal has been said and written in times past about the "weaker sex." If men are not capable of taking care of themselves during periods of stress and unemployment, does parliament think women are more capable of taking care of themselves?' Despite the evidence that thousands of women had no one to support them and that many also had dependants whom they could not support, legislators suggested that women could always 'be absorbed in family life or housework.' The belief persisted that women need not be unemployed because they could supposedly obtain work, together with room and board, as live-in domestic servants. Beleaguered legislators could, in any event, ignore the plight of single, unemployed women more readily since they were seen as far less likely than men to organize or resort to violence.

It thus fell to women reformers, together with labour activists and a few women politicians, to speak up for unemployed women. Women's organizations continued to lobby for effective government action, and some also developed their own aid schemes. In 1930, for example, the Vancouver Local Council of Women undertook to find jobs, housing, and meals for unemployed females. The council also brought these females' need for work or relief to the attention of municipal authorities and mounted a newspaper campaign urging employers to give them jobs. The council convinced a volunteer 'make-work' organization to include women in its program and also helped the YWCA set up a workroom for the female unemployed.

Yet, under the 1937 Dominion-Provincial Youth Training Programme, new policy to combat female unemployment relied on an age-old solution: training in domestic service through urban schools. In addition to classroom instruction, the young women cooked, cleaned, scrubbed, and did laundry and other household tasks, sometimes in private homes. The goal of the Home Service Training Course was to convince young women to choose this type of employment and prepare them for their 'ultimate occupation of homemakers.' The program was aimed at dependent girls from respectable families on relief, but the status of this occupation was so low that the preferred candidates were reluctant to take the training. Many others left in summer when seasonal employment became available. Only a limited number of young women received this training, and less than half were placed in employment.

As the ravages of the Depression continued, married women's home production became increasingly important not only to stretch scant wages or relief payments but also to increase the family income. For example, when the Lekwammen of Vancouver Island found the sources of wage labour drying up in the 1930s, they shifted back to an emphasis on subsistence and on women's home production. While Lekwammen women were sometimes still able to earn a little money picking hops and berries, cannery jobs became scarce. Consequently, the women's production of hand-knit sweaters became especially important to generate income. The knitting could be done during the seasons when there was not much other work, and, like non-Aboriginal mothers who took in sewing from clothing contractors in a very different context, Lekwammen mothers could combine this kind of home-based income earning with childrearing. Other members of Lekwammen families could also help with the production of sweaters.

More than during times of fuller employment, many non-Aboriginal women similarly came to rely increasingly on home-based needlework (including embroidery, knitting, dressmaking, and braiding rugs) to raise cash for their families. The shortage of cash was sometimes so severe that women's skills in 'making do' became crucial. Some women resorted to using flour sacks to make clothing for their families, took in washing, or sold baked goods. Even in cases of extreme poverty, reluctance to overturn entrenched gender roles may have led some married women to choose these measures instead of searching for jobs in the paid labour force if their husbands were unemployed.

Thus, amid all the fear that women's paid work was damaging in so many ways, their employment patterns changed relatively little during this difficult decade. A significant number of women were apparently able to retain their positions in the paid labour force in the 1930s both because many women's economic needs were hard to deny and, ironically, because they still 'only' did 'women's work.'

PART II

Confronting the Disjuncture

4

Social Reform and Regulation

The massive social problems that accompanied rapid industrialization and urbanization in Canada in the late nineteenth and early twentieth centuries aroused the consciences of many middle-class Canadians. Social reformers were often especially concerned about the plight of women and children in the paid workforce. Their concerns were paternalistic – they supposed women to be nearly as helpless as children and therefore in need of male protection. In part, it was the disjuncture between notions of proper womanhood and the actual treatment of women workers that aroused their concern and spurred them to press for protective measures. The reformers used maternalist discourse to justify their goals. In the laissez-faire climate of the times, there were people who generally opposed state intervention in the labour market but who were nonetheless willing to call for legislation to protect the nation's 'future mothers.'

In fact, since women had habitually performed hard labour on struggling family farms in the pre-industrial period, fears about their physical frailty arose not from an examination of their capacity to perform such work in general but rather from intense anxieties about their employment in new industries and commercial establishments. Reformers pointed to the fumes, heat, and noise in factories, as well as the speed of new machines, as endangering the physical and mental health of future mothers. In the case of shops, standing for long hours was believed to be damaging to women's procreative capacities. As we shall see, reformers were just as worried that women's moral purity was imperilled, as these women were leaving the presumed protection of their families and working in close contact with strange men in factories and shops. Paid employment would prevent young, single women from learning adequate domestic skills from their mothers, reformers feared, while preventing married women from fulfilling their domestic functions properly. The reformers believed that certain forms of work, especially in factories, would coarsen women's allegedly finer natures and undermine their femininity.

'Protecting' Women Workers

Some of the social reformers who tackled these issues, such as Dr Darby Bergin, a physician representing the industrializing town of Cornwall in the House of Commons in the late nineteenth century, were members of the growing liberal professions. Such men – and the few women who succeeded in overcoming so many obstacles to enter these professions – had great confidence in their own expertise and in their ability to eliminate the worst problems of urban, industrial society through social and political action.

Bergin was one of the first advocates of legislation to protect women workers in Canada. His concern for working-class welfare originated with his work as a physician during an outbreak of typhoid among Irish immigrants in Cornwall. His proposals for factory legislation to protect women and children in the early 1880s foreshadowed the emergence of wide-ranging public concern over these problems in Canada. In fact, Bergin was anticipating some of the negative social consequences of industrialization in light of developments in Great Britain and the United States. Hence he called for preventive legislation in Canada. Drawing on studies by American physicians, Bergin warned that the 'constant standing and the constant heat of and confinement in the mills' damaged women's reproductive organs. The Cornwall MP also believed that factory work rendered women morally unfit for motherhood. Although the federal government established a commission in response to Bergin's early impassioned calls for protective legislation, no legislation was enacted at that time.

Concerns about the effects of factory work on 'proper womanhood' also shaped the investigation and recommendations of the middle-class members of the Royal Commission on the Relations of Labour and Capital, appointed in 1887 by Prime Minister John A. Macdonald. A wave of labour unrest at that time had motivated Macdonald to establish the commission to examine industrial conditions in Canada. Labour activists, some of whom were appointed to the commission, were concerned above all with the material conditions of working people and, unlike the middle-class commissioners, did not assume that female workers could be easily corrupted morally. But morality was the main preoccupation of the middle-class commissioners in their investigation of the condition of female factory workers and shop assistants. In questioning various witnesses about the situation of women workers, they focused on whether females were exposed to coarse language, whether toilet facilities were segregated by sex, and whether male employers and supervisors abused the females physically or sexually. In contrast, their questions to and about male workers were confined to economic and political matters such as wages, hours, deskilling, and the role of unions. Although these commissioners concluded that no 'serious immorality' existed in 'Canadian factories in which operatives of both sexes are employed,' they recommended that female inspectors be appointed to visit factories in which women were employed, and that Ottawa enact laws to protect girls 'approaching womanhood' from 'severe or long continued work' so as to safeguard their ability to bear children.

For reformers like the young William Lyon Mackenzie

King, concerns about the plight of female workers stemmed from religious motivations. Born into a devout Presbyterian family, King desired to put Christian principles into practice, even as an adolescent, by helping the poor and underprivileged. His university studies and his experiences at Hull House, Jane Addams's famous settlement house in Chicago's slums, further stimulated his reform orientation. As a reporter for the Toronto *Mail and Empire* in the late 1890s, King became aware of – and then exposed – the plight of female garment workers in the city's 'sweating' system, which he described in his diary as 'a story of Hell.' He then convinced the federal government to regulate hours, wages, and sanitary conditions among the manufacturers who produced mail bags and postal uniforms. In 1907, then Canada's deputy minister of labour, King joined a commission appointed to investigate the conditions of female Bell telephone operators in the wake of a strike against Bell in Toronto. By this point, concern about the childbearing capacities of female workers had all but eclipsed his awareness of their economic plight. The commission relied very heavily on the testimony of medical 'experts' about the effects of long hours and technical equipment on the health of the telephone operators, and the resulting report criticized Bell for 'working women at high pressure.' King likened Bell to a 'hideous octopus feeding upon the life blood of young women and girls.' Bell's employment practices changed little, however.

Some employers, worried about their public image, instituted paternalistic welfare measures for their employees. While they sometimes extended similar benefits to male and female workers (such as financial assistance during illness and the use of company libraries, sitting rooms, and gyms), paternalism towards female employees emphasized male authority and female obedience and dependence. The fatherly employer would look after 'his girls,' sometimes taking special measures to safeguard his female employees' morality. For example, at a Peterborough clock factory towards the end of the period under consideration, male managers took care to hire only 'good girls, respectable girls,' and took other steps to protect their reputations, such as providing advice about 'ladylike' clothing.

As Women for Women's Sake

Social reformers could not simply rely on employers' paternalism to protect women workers. In contrast to reformers like King, who discovered the plight of women workers as a result of broader concerns about the impact of industrialization on Canadian society, many female reformers believed that 'as women' they had a special responsibility to act 'for the sake of women.' For the same reason, their male counterparts also believed that women were uniquely equipped to deal with the problems of labouring women and children. Whatever their motivation, middle-class female reformers penned some of the most detailed and interesting accounts of the conditions of women workers at the turn of the twentieth century. The earliest of these was a scholarly study written in 1892 by Jean Scott, one of a growing number of Canadian women who were attending university in the late nineteenth century. Two decades later, Maude Pettit, another university graduate and an employee of Methodist Publications, adopted a far more unorthodox method of obtaining information on the lives of female workers by disguising herself as a 'factory girl' and taking on a series of typical 'women's jobs' in this capacity. She disclosed her findings through a month-long series of articles in the *Toronto Star* in 1912. In conjunction with such studies, female reformers pushed for measures to improve the lot of female employees. In Winnipeg, for example, Nellie McClung and other feminists took the premier of Manitoba to various factories to convince him of the need for reforms on behalf of women, while the University Women's Club investigated the situation of women working in the city's department stores.

Yet the activists in women's groups did not always display such concern about women workers. In fact, in the late nineteenth century, Lady Ishbel Aberdeen, president of the National Council of Women of Canada (NCWC), had warned a council member not to focus on the plight of female garment workers because to do so would 'arouse the wrath of some trades-people.' In 1901, the NCWC explicitly denied that Canada had a problem with the use of the sweating system to produce clothing, despite investigations by King and others.

Those female activists who were particularly concerned about the plight of women workers spearheaded a debate that continues to engage feminists to this day: was full legal equality the only means to ensure the equality of women in society, or was differential legal treatment called for since women are the bearers of children? This question shaped discussions about the advisability of protective labour legislation for women. The debate within the NCWC emerged in the 1890s when social critic Agnes Maule Machar proposed that the council call for legislation to restrict women's work day to nine hours. She argued that the state should protect women because they lacked the capacity to organize against their own exploitation. She also maintained that protective legislation would not privilege women over men since 'the heaviest burden rests' on women and children, 'the burden of the longest hours, the smallest pay, the harshest and most unreasonable exaction.'

Yet as another NCWC member pointed out, shorter hours could actually harm women workers by cutting into their earnings. The council was being asked, she argued, 'to decide between the physical deterioration of the mothers of our nation on the one hand or their starvation on the other.' While some opponents of protective legislation apparently believed that the state should not interfere with the employer's 'right' to hire whomever he pleased, Carrie Derick, another NCWC member and a McGill University professor, opposed protective legislation on the grounds of both principle and practice. She rejected the very idea of legislation based on differences between men and women. She argued that it was inherently contradictory to proclaim 'the equality of women with men and their right to compete with them, and [proclaim] at the same time ... that special privileges be accorded them on account of [their] inability to bear the same burdens.' In practical terms, she also believed that legislation designed to protect women specifically could be damaging for the very group it sought to protect. Restricting the hours of women's employment would mean that some women would lose their jobs, for employers would replace them with boys.

Lady Julia Drummond, an NCWC member who was the wife of the president of the Bank of Montreal, believed that legislation designed to protect women workers would harm them in the long run by stereotyping them as weak. Employers could invoke women's frailty to justify paying them lower wages and restricting them to certain occupations. Lady Drummond was also critical of male support for protective legislation. She argued that fear of competition from women workers, rather than concern for their welfare, led male unionists to support protective legislation for women. These males, Lady Drummond believed, hoped that measures such as shorter hours for women would lead employers to reduce the use of female employees.

Many of these opponents of protective legislation for women believed that the position of female workers could be improved through laws reducing hours for all workers and through legal guarantees of equal pay for equal work. But deeply ingrained attitudes against state intervention in the 'freedom of contract' between employers and employees meant that, as we shall see, the introduction – and then enforcement – of laws that would improve the lot of all workers would prove difficult.

The Biases of Women Reformers

The middle-class background of most social reformers could prevent them from grasping some of the problems of employed working-class women and helping them on their own terms. Even as young women by the thousands showed a clear preference for factory work over domestic service, many reformers insisted that domestic service offered the best solution for women who needed to earn money. So wedded were they to this view that they disregarded the reasons for the intense dislike of domestic service, including the problem of sexual harassment. No doubt their own difficulty in finding servants partly explains their tireless promotion of this occupation. But suspicion of the character of wage-earning women was just as important, for they feared that female factory workers would become too independent, and thus endanger their morals. In addition, arguments favouring domestic service could be strengthened by linking them to the good of the nation: through such employment young women, whose fertility might otherwise be damaged by factory work, could be prepared to assume their ultimate responsibility as mothers.

Reformer Constance Hamilton, wife of a prominent Canadian Pacific Railway official, promoted the idea of limiting domestics' working hours to ten per day, despite the self-sacrifice that this would require from women with only one or two maids. 'Our duty to the race demands,' she explained, 'that we should govern the conditions of this young woman's work so that in later years she may have a chance of becoming the mother of a second generation.' Local branches of the NCWC and the Young Women's Christian Association (YWCA) offered domestic science courses in an attempt to elevate the status of both homemaking and domestic service and thus discourage women from working in factories.

Some of the same suffragists who demanded the right to vote so that they could defend women and children in the paid labour force, snubbed those working-class women whom they met, frowning on their poor clothing and ungrammatical speech. Local branches of the NCWC were no more receptive to these women. Although the Trades and Labour

Congress of Canada (the main umbrella organization for unions in this country) appointed fraternal delegates to local NCWC branches, these union delegates were largely ignored. Some reformers held deeply patronizing attitudes towards employed working-class women. They assumed that by virtue of their own greater education and class position they were better able to judge what was good for these women than were the women workers themselves. Indeed, this was one reason why middle-class reformers favoured government regulation to improve the conditions of women's work.

Class biases also surfaced in the copious attention that middle-class, female reformers paid to working-class women's leisure pursuits, at a time when employers had a vested interest in the creation of a sober, well-disciplined workforce. While some of these reformers wanted to protect women workers, whom they saw as helpless innocents, others were deeply suspicious of women workers' moral character. Reformers saw confirmation of their suspicions in the fact that many working-class women chose dirty factory work over domestic service, presumably partly in order to have more time for 'cheap amusements' in dance halls, vaudeville houses, amusement parks, and other unchaperoned settings. Whether they saw female workers as innocent and vulnerable or as morally weak, reformers felt that these women should not be left on their own in the city. Cities, they believed, were full of vice, and a young woman could easily be ensnared by 'white slavers,' sex fiends, and drug pushers. The media promoted sensationalist stories portraying vicious males, many of them Asian immigrants (depicted as opium-smoking 'degenerates' from China) or Jews or African Canadians, corrupting previously respectable young women.

From this point of view, employed working-class women required supervision by their social superiors. To protect them from the dangers of seduction, prostitution, sexually transmitted diseases, and drug or alcohol addiction, female reformers attempted to substitute 'healthy recreation' for cheap commercial entertainments. They established reading rooms, gymnasia, tennis courts, working women's clubs, and supervised dances, as they campaigned against such things as 'immoral' clothing fashions and 'immoral' movies. Some of the programs for 'improving' women workers were based on the assumption that the inadequacies of these females – their lack of education and special skills – were the main reasons for their marginalization in the labour force. Reformers hoped that through better education these women could be 'uplifted.'

Women reformers in the YWCA and other groups also established supervised boarding houses especially for young women who were coming to urban centres in search of jobs. This initiative was designed to protect the young women from the city's temptations, but these houses did not cater to the neediest female workers. Admission was frequently restricted to young, white, Protestant women with spotless reputations. By the early twentieth century, most of their residents were 'businesswomen' (mainly 'office girls'). The residences offered practical advantages such as prepared meals and laundry facilities, as well as 'rational recreations,' but they also curtailed the autonomy of the inhabitants. Indeed, the houses were intended to replicate strict familial control over their residents. The women were required to keep their rooms tidy, to return home by a reasonable hour, and to ask permission to entertain guests. In some cases, they were required to attend prayer meetings.

Efforts to 'protect' women in the paid labour force sometimes took overtly racist turns. In the early twentieth century, some social reformers campaigned for laws to prohibit immigrant Chinese males from employing 'white women' in their small businesses (such as restaurants and laundries). In this period, racist stereotypes portrayed immigrant Chinese men as sexual predators who lured 'white women' to ruin. If the women themselves did not know better than to work for such lecherous and devious men, argued the reformers, the law should step in and protect them. In the campaigns for such a 'White Women's Labour Law,' various Protestant clergymen and other male reformers were joined by a variety of female reformers, including representatives of the Woman's Christian Temperance Union (WCTU), the Young Women's Christian Association, and the National Council of Women of Canada. Emily Murphy, a prominent feminist who was Canada's first female magistrate, actively promoted such sensationalist racist views. Although Helen Gregory MacGill, another prominent feminist and also a judge, argued that the law should protect female workers from sexual exploitation without singling out a particular race, several provinces passed such legislation under pressure not only from social reformers but also from racist white businessmen and labour leaders, who feared competition from immigrant Chinese males.

With only a few exceptions, middle-class female reformers seldom looked to the labour movement to fight for women workers. Indeed, many opposed women's participation in unions. During early industrialization, middle-class women opposed strikes, partly for humanitarian considerations and partly from a naive faith in peaceful arbitration of employers' and workers' interests. The Fédération Nationale Saint-Jean-Baptiste (FNSJB), a prominent French-Canadian women's organization in the early twentieth century believed that the aggressive manner of unions was 'not at all compatible with the peaceful role a woman must play in the political economy, even when it involves demonstrating her own just demands.' Members of the FNSJB also feared that unions would undermine another element of 'proper womanhood' – piety. To prevent 'neutral, socialist or openly anti-clerical' unions from making inroads among Quebec women, French-Canadian women reformers established 'professional associations' for women employees of factories, stores, and offices. Each of these associations had its own chaplain, who was to nurture the spiritual development of the women, and an upper-middle-class patron. Madame Rolland, wife of the president of the Canadian

Manufacturers' Association, was the patron for factory employees, while the patron for store employees was Madame Dupuis, wife of the owner of Dupuis Frères, a large Montreal department store. Marie Gérin-Lajoie, a leading Quebec feminist, explained the role of these patrons: 'If we have the wives of our Employers with us and on our side, we will be surer of obtaining a hearing and it will doubtless be easier to obtain certain reforms.'

Each association was to resemble an extended family, concerned about a combination of economic and moral issues. Fédération leaders hoped that the working-class women within these organizations would be morally uplifted and would, in turn, be able to elevate other female workers morally. The associations provided mutual aid, especially a fund for those who were sick. The association of factory workers pressed employers to comply with religious holidays, to improve lighting, and to hire female supervisors to safeguard the women from the sexual advances of unscrupulous male supervisors. In addition to providing domestic science courses, the FNSJB also provided employment bureaus and boarding houses for the female factory workers. The organization chalked up some important concrete gains. The Professional Association of Office Employees helped defeat a bill that would have prohibited women from becoming Superior Court stenographers, and the teachers' association helped increase women teachers' pensions. At the same time, the FNSJB continued its moralistic orientation, and it carefully distinguished between the 'professional association' and unions, which it still rejected.

Alice Chown discovered the distance between middle-class women's organizations and the labour movement when she tried to mobilize support for a large strike at Eaton's Toronto garment factory in 1912. Although Chown was a product of an Anglo-Celtic, middle-class upbringing, her concern for social reform atypically led her to become increasingly radical. 'I tried to interest the various women's clubs [to support the Eaton strikers],' she wrote, 'but I was amazed because they had no sympathy with the strikers, unless I had some tale of hardship to tell. The common, everyday longings for better conditions, for a life that would provide more than food, clothes and shelter, were not recognized as justifying a strike. I had to tell over and over the old, old story of the bosses who favored the girls whom they could take out evenings, girls who had to sell themselves as well as their labor to get sufficient work to earn a living.' Even this emphasis on sexual harassment brought little support. After all, most of the Eaton's strikers were immigrant Jews from eastern Europe, and in these years the Canadian women's movement was steeped in prejudice, explicitly proclaiming Christian (indeed often specifically Protestant) values. Jews were viewed as a threat and even as immoral. (The WCTU's newspaper went so far as to reprint anti-Jewish material from Henry Ford's viciously anti-Semitic *Dearborn Independent*.) In such a climate, ethnic divisions sometimes deepened the gulf between middle-class reformers and female workers.

At times, middle-class women's organizations took distinctly anti-labour positions in the midst of women's strikes. Winnipeg's Local Council of Women, for example, attacked the Woolworth sales clerks' strike in 1917, as well as the civic workers' strike a year later. At one point in 1918, a group of council women actually served as strikebreakers, replacing militant telephone operators. Wartime patriotism no doubt intensified their lack of sympathy for women strikers. Around the same time, labour activists also criticized Calgary's Local Council of Women for not supporting the reinstatement of female laundry workers who had been fired for unionizing.

Most often, middle-class groups remained neutral or indifferent in the midst of such strikes. Even when middle-class suffragists took the unusual step of providing some assistance to female strikers during the large Montreal clothing strike of 1910, they carefully announced that they would 'take no active part in the present strike which might give the impression that they were siding with the strikers against the employers.' The atypical support that middle-class women's organizations offered to a small group of female dressmakers in 1934 was the product of the way the Royal Commission on Price Spreads and Mass Buying had crystallized public opinion against the T. Eaton Company.

In Canada, there was no group similar to the Women's Trade Union League (WTUL) in the United States. Founded in 1903 and consisting of a cross-class and interethnic alliance of women, the WTUL sought to improve the conditions of American women workers by working with the established labour movement and by pushing for protective labour legislation. In cities such as New York and Chicago, the WTUL succeeded for a time in mobilizing significant middle-class, female support for the union activities of women workers, especially in the clothing industry. The absence of a similar organization in Canada, despite a couple of attempts to establish one, indicates that few early-twentieth-century Canadian women reformers were prepared to support a union-oriented approach to the problems of women workers. Canada's female workers thus had less opportunity than their American counterparts to become effectively integrated into the movement for women's rights.

On the whole, Canada's middle-class female reformers sought only modest measures to remedy some of the worst excesses of the new industrial system. They sought such provisions as separate washrooms for women, the appointment of female factory inspectors (with whom women workers would more readily discuss their problems), and lunchrooms so that women would not have to eat their lunches on the street in all kinds of weather. Many of them condescended towards women workers, particularly as they sought to supervise the women's morals. Class biases meshed with racist attitudes in the campaigns for 'white women's labour laws.' Reformers' sense of responsibility for the fate of their less fortunate counterparts manifested itself primarily in greater vigilance in ensuring the enforcement of laws enacted to protect women workers.

Factory Laws

Labour unrest in the 1880s, rather than reformers' efforts, was the decisive factor behind the state's initial steps to protect blue-collar workers. Ontario and Quebec introduced the first factory acts in 1884 and 1885, respectively, to be followed later in the Maritimes and the West. All these statutes rested on the assumption that female workers needed greater protection than male workers because of their presumed physical frailty and moral vulnerability.

The provisions and application of the Ontario Factories' Act illustrate the significance of protective legislation for women workers. It provided some protection for all workers by establishing minimum standards for safety, cleanliness, and ventilation, and preventing overcrowding. Above all, it aimed to help the most vulnerable – women and children. Night work for women was prohibited, and their working hours were restricted to a maximum of ten per day and sixty per week. Employers also had to give women an hour off for lunch (not to be counted as one of their ten working hours). Women could not be employed to clean machinery in motion or, more broadly, in factories where their health was 'likely to be permanently injured.' Employers also had to provide separate toilets for male and female employees. The law was amended in 1890, making it a criminal offence for employers or supervisors in factories, mills, and workshops to seduce female employees 'of previously chaste character' under the age of twenty-one. In 1888, Ontario also passed legislation to protect female shop employees; eventually the other provinces did the same. In view of the prevailing medical opinion that women's health, in particular their reproductive capacity, would be damaged by prolonged standing, saleswomen were to be provided with chairs so that they could sit when not engaged with customers.

These laws made very little practical difference in women's work lives. By the time the legislation was enacted in Ontario, many women did not work longer than the legislated number of hours. Few women sought to avail themselves of the guaranteed time off for lunch, as it would be added to a very long working day. Since additional work awaited them at home, most women preferred to eat quickly by their machines so they could begin attending to their domestic duties as early as possible. Moreover, there were many loopholes in the factory laws. They applied, at first, only to places with over twenty employees, and special provisions allowed employers to require women to work overtime 'when the customs or exigencies' of the trade required. The laws also proved difficult to enforce. Reformers who investigated the impact of the Shops Act, for instance, discovered that employers observed the letter of the law by providing seats for saleswomen, but they did not allow the women to use these seats. Afraid of losing their jobs, saleswomen did not complain about their employers' hypocrisy. Factory inspectors in Ontario, as elsewhere, were too few in number to ensure that legislative provisions were observed. Even if inspectors caught violators, the fines they could impose were too low to function as effective deterrents. Precisely because these laws were so limited and ineffective, they did not generally discourage employers from hiring women.

But these protective labour laws did have significant negative effects – symbolic and otherwise – for women workers in the long term. By giving official recognition to women as a distinct, dependent category of workers in need of state protection, the laws set the stage for further legislation that would continue to restrict women's opportunities in the workforce. The emphasis on protecting women's childbearing capacities buttressed the view that women's primary role was as the bearers and rearers of children and hence that their participation in the paid labour force was temporary and of secondary importance. The protective labour laws also reinforced gender segregation in the workplace by underlining the presumed differences between male and female workers. The laws legitimated the view that there were certain types of jobs that women could not do. Thus they contributed to the divisions between male and female workers, potentially decreasing male-female solidarity in the labour movement.

Minimum Wage Laws for Women

During the final years of the First World War, social reformers from groups such as the National Council of Women of Canada first advocated minimum wage legislation to counteract low wages paid to women workers. By 1922, most provinces had introduced minimum wage laws specifically for women, after investigations confirmed that many women did not earn enough to support themselves. Provincial minimum wage boards were established to set the minimum rates.

The war intensified anxieties about the physical wellbeing of future mothers. Was there a link between the poor physical condition of military recruits and the growth in the number of female factory workers since the late nineteenth century? Even more women were entering the industrial workforce, and some of them performed 'men's' work in heavy industry. Fears of 'race suicide' (the notion that the allegedly superior race would die out as alleged inferiors reproduced rapidly) were also fuelled by the very high casualty rate among the Canadian forces. Anglo-Celtic Canadians noted with alarm and anger that men of 'foreign' extraction remained in Canada and supposedly reaped the benefits of a soaring wartime economy. The loss of so many men of marrying age, moreover, meant that many women would be unable to marry and would therefore have to depend on their own wages. Male workers' fears of competition from women workers who replaced enlisted men, together with workers' militancy during the war, also forced middle-class Canadians to pay more attention to the condition of women workers.

The initial decision to set minimum wages only for females was itself a compromise with employers and helped perpetuate gender inequality in the labour force. Employers maintained that the contract between management and male workers was between equals, and hence there was no room for state intervention. They firmly opposed minimum wages for men. But the belief that women needed special protection spurred the acceptance of minimum wage legislation for women workers at that time. The traditional gender ideology led boards to set minimum wages very low. The Ontario Board, for example, set especially low wages for female minors and learners because of the presumption that they could depend on their fathers. At the same time, the board assumed that all women workers over eighteen were single and supported only themselves. It therefore set minimum wages substantially lower than the earnings of unskilled male workers, who were believed to have dependants. Although this was a step beyond conventional assumptions that women worked only for 'pin money,' board members clearly ignored the findings of their own investigators that many women workers were supporting others beside themselves. Moreover, no allowance was made for cyclical layoffs, illness, or vacations. The 'working girl' ought to be content with modest means appropriate to her class. Not for her the frivolity of fine dress, jewellery, or commercial entertainments, which were, in any event, morally suspect in the eyes of reformers. Indeed, her need to manage on a tight budget would develop her moral fibre.

Many women were denied even these meagre wages. Large categories of wage-earning women, such as domestics and farm workers, were not covered by the legislation. Employers could evade minimum wage regulations without too much difficulty, especially because there were so few inspectors and because women feared losing their jobs if they reported violations. Employers wishing to observe the letter of the law could rely on an ever-changing workforce of 'learners' or on part-time workers who could be paid less than the standard minimum. In the case of women who were on piece rates, employers had to pay only 80 per cent of them the 'minimum' wage. Hence management could easily claim that those women who made less than the 'minimum' had only their own inefficiency to blame. In addition, during periods of downturn in different trades, employers were exempted from paying the legal minimum if it would necessitate layoffs. Finally, since fines were seldom imposed, they did not carry much force as deterrents.

Despite these serious shortcomings, women's organizations, whose members served on some minimum wage boards, seemed well pleased with the new legislation. Their continuing belief that other issues, such as industrial sanitation, were of far greater significance to female workers' well-being than was the question of wages, may explain women reformers' insensitivity to the legislation's defects. But some reformers, such as the members of the Calgary Local Council of Women, also held on to the notion – yet again – that domestic service was, in any case, a more suitable occupation than factory work for working-class women.

The problems with women's minimum wage legislation increased during the Great Depression. The worst fears of those who had opposed minimum wage laws came to pass when some employers fired women to replace them with men who were driven by the economic crisis to work for wages lower than the women's minimum. More often, employers who retained their female employees exploited the looming threat of unemployment to circumvent minimum wage laws even more blatantly than during the 1920s. Most provinces expanded their minimum wage laws in the mid-1930s to encompass men as well. But problems enforcing these laws remained.

Mothers' Allowances

Reformers from various women's groups believed that the domestic ideology would be buttressed among the 'lower classes' by supporting impoverished mothers who were, through no fault of their own, raising children alone. Feminists such as Flora MacDonald Denison thus advocated paying such poor mothers a wage so they would be free to care for their children themselves. The National Council of Women had discussed this type of legislation as early as 1899. By 1914, the Toronto Local Council of Women established its own pilot project to pay needy widows with young children in order to demonstrate the importance and the feasibility of mothers' allowances. More broadly, the First World War not only heightened awareness of maternal care as important for the health of the nation, but also left many families fatherless and in need of assistance. The experience of volunteers from the Canadian Patriotic Fund distributing funds to 'deserving' mothers in needy families of soldiers fighting overseas, proved crucial to designing the new system of mothers' allowances. Mothers' allowances laws were instituted in seven provinces, beginning with the Prairie provinces towards the end of the war.

Such legislation was both innovative and confining. For some, it represented public recognition of the value of women's unpaid work. Thus pioneer social worker Charlotte Whitton explained that 'mothers' aid is not generally regarded as relief or charity but as remuneration by the state to the mother for caring for her children.' Yet such legislation also reinforced notions of women's dependence. The state was stepping in, in the place of husbands, to support women whose primary duty was to raise children. Discontinuing aid when children turned sixteen indicated that the state's concern was not with the welfare of mothers but rather with that of future workers and citizens. Without specialized skills and work experience and bereft of state support once their children were grown, women who had depended on mothers' allowance faced the prospect of great economic hardship.

Class was also an important dimension. Although this aid was not charity but payment for services 'to the state by bringing up of its citizens,' suspicions did not disappear concerning the moral weaknesses of the impoverished women who rendered this important public service. Significant groups of women who were bringing up children on their own did not qualify for support. In many cases, a widow who had only one child was ineligible, not only because of the state's desire to cut costs but also because of the social reformers' assumption that she should be able to obtain work as a live-in domestic servant, accompanied by her child, in a respectable middle-class home. In addition, unwed mothers were generally deemed unworthy of aid because they had engaged in sexual activity outside marriage. Consequently, in most provinces, only widows or the wives of disabled men were deemed eligible for assistance. Doubts concerning deserted wives also rendered them ineligible for mothers' allowances everywhere but in British Columbia.

Those deemed eligible for assistance were assumed to need the guiding hand of middle-class social workers in carrying out their maternal duties properly. They had to demonstrate their deservingness through cleanliness, industriousness, thrift, and similar behaviour. Investigators visited their homes to ensure that the mothers' morality was unimpeachable and that the children were being well brought up and were attending school regularly. Of course, respectable mothers were not to drink, swear, or carry on with men. If possible, the mother should have 'a look of hope and contentment on [her] face' when the investigator arrived. Only the truly moral mother was to receive the allowance.

Allowances were also deliberately set too low to permit women and their children to survive on them alone. The head of the Ontario Mothers' Allowance Commission worried in 1924 that 'full maintenance ... would create wastefulness and probably laziness.' The remunerative work that was encouraged was familiar to poverty-stricken mothers: homework (particularly in the garment industry) that permitted them to stay at home and combine earnings with child rearing but that also yielded low income.

'Foreign' – that is, non-Anglo-Celtic – mothers faced particular scrutiny. The program administrators believed that, unlike truly Canadian widows, 'foreigners' could manage to support their children on earnings from such seasonal labour as fruit picking, presumably because they were accustomed to a lower standard of living. Some were formally excluded. Recipients were expected to be British subjects and to meet strict residency requirements. Recent immigrants who had not had time to become naturalized and whose families frequently moved around in search of work could thus not qualify.

Racism hit hardest in British Columbia. Because the proportion of 'whites' was smaller there, fears about being outnumbered by non-Anglo-Celtic groups were more intense and resulted in more value being accorded to women bearing Anglo-Celtic babies. Hence, in BC deserted wives were eligible for mothers' allowances, and even unwed mothers could qualify. At the same time, non-Anglo-Celtic women, especially those of Asian background, were much more likely to be excluded.

During the Great Depression, women on mothers' allowance found it harder to find jobs to supplement this income. Even if they did find work, they frequently faced hostility from women not eligible for assistance. Children over the age of sixteen were also less able to find work to help their mothers. They frequently stayed in school and depended on their mothers longer. Yet governments of all levels did little to assist even these women who had officially qualified as 'vulnerable.' Partly in response to pressure from the labour movement, some provinces eventually extended mothers' allowances to cover mothers of children up to eighteen. At the same time, investigation of applicants grew stricter, and more applicants were turned down.

Conclusion

In general, from the late nineteenth century through the 1930s, various male and female social reformers struggled to soften some of the harshest blows of industrial capitalism for the weakest and most vulnerable. Despite minor improvements, the overall results were meagre. Many of the legislative changes that reformers had struggled to achieve turned out to be mainly ineffective. The potential for more meaningful change was limited not only by stereotyped notions of womanhood, combined with concrete economic interests, but also by the reformers' own class and ethnic biases. The vast majority of social reformers did not envision more fundamental change, and the exigencies of industrial capitalism were so often relentless.

5

Resistance and Its Limits

'With a union when we return to work [after winning this strike,] there will be no need to bring kegs of wine, cakes and chicken for the bosses. You won't have to be good looking to get a break,' declared Mary Jary. 'You won't have to listen to some of that awful language we hear in the mill. The union would give everyone a fair chance and they would receive treatment like humans, not like cattle.'

It was December 1936, and over eight hundred employees of the Empire Cotton Mills in Welland, Ontario, had walked off the job. More than half the strikers were women, and Mary Jary, a Hungarian Canadian, was one of the most active. These women and men were protesting against wages so low and working conditions so unacceptable that Ontario's Liberal minister of labour denounced the company for fomenting labour unrest by its 'shameful underpayment and exploitation of workers.' Women were every bit as militant as men in this dramatic, month-long strike, behaving in ways that were completely at odds with prescriptions for 'proper womanhood.' Together with the men, women picketed the mill day and night, taking turns warming up in front of a makeshift fire. Female picketers accosted mill supervisors to prevent them from loading trucks with textiles. In response, police struck the women with their batons.

Jary gave impassioned speeches, which at times brought tears to the eyes of her listeners. She defied the domestic ideology both in action and in words. About two weeks into the strike, she asked reporters: 'What do you think of our spirit now – haven't we got the light of battle in our eyes?' She also announced defiantly that she would continue to march on the picket line despite the fact that she had a three-year-old son at home.

Jary, whose husband also worked at the Empire Cotton Mills, supported both the strike and the United Textile Workers without questioning the discrepancy in wages paid men and women at the mill. Asked whether employees could live on the wages they received, she responded: 'If I died my husband would have to get another woman to help him make a living.' She viewed the workers' struggle from the perspective of the family as a whole, rather than in more gendered terms.

As we have seen, the social reformers' efforts at labour reform were often premised on the belief that women workers were too weak to protect themselves, but Jary's outspoken militancy indicates that women workers did indeed stand up for themselves on occasion. Given the labour movement's blue-collar orientation, factory women were particularly important in this respect. But, as we shall see, militancy also took place at times among women who were telephone operators, hotel maids, waitresses, laundry workers, and even sales clerks. Meanwhile, the more professional white-collar workers took their own steps to improve their status and earnings. Class and ethnic divisions among employed women made it difficult for them to cooperate in their endeavours. All employed women, moreover, faced barriers that limited the possibilities of protest. This is partly why protests in specific occupations and workplaces did not coalesce into broadly based campaigns to end discrimination against women in the paid labour force in the period under consideration.

The labour movement as a whole remained fairly weak throughout these years. Unions were often unable to hold their own in the face of employer aggression. Until the

Second World War, there was no comprehensive legal framework to guarantee the right to collective bargaining. Even
when a union demonstrated that it had majority support in
a particular workplace, the employer usually did not have to
recognize or enter into collective bargaining with the union.
The courts and the police often sided with the employers.
In fact, state repression sometimes took violent forms, especially when troops were called in to put down a strike. In
this context, unions signed up only a small proportion of
male wage earners. Women workers faced many barriers
that limited protest, some of which they shared with men,
especially the less skilled. The women generally faced additional obstacles as well.

Domesticity, Femininity, and Respectability

How much did ideological constraints inhibit protest by
women who went out to work? Not all women were like
Mary Jary, and, even in the blue-collar sector, some young
women workers hoped soon to become full-time housewives and hesitated to invest time and energy in workplace
protests or in the labour movement itself. As a male labour
representative explained in 1895, bemoaning women's reluctance to agitate for higher pay: 'In too many cases [women
workers] look to marriage as the door through which they
will escape from toil, and not expecting to be permanently
in the labour market, they do not insist on keeping it up to
a high standard.' Over three decades later, a prominent
female Communist Party organizer regretted that 'women
do not take wage earning seriously. To them it is only a
temporary necessity.'

Under widespread social pressure to obey men, some
women faced other social inhibitions in their struggles
against male employers. They worried that unions were not
respectable for proper young ladies. Thus Leonora Barry,
general investigator of women's work for the Knights of
Labor and organizer of women workers in both Canada and

the United States, reported in the late 1880s that her attempts to organize women floundered because of 'the habit of submission ... foolish pride, prudish modesty and religious scruples; and ... the hope and expectancy that in the near future marriage will lift them out of the industrial life to the quiet and comfort of a home.' Another woman worker in the late nineteenth century declared: 'Organization ... was all very well, but how were girls to accomplish it; were they to advertise mass meetings, mount platforms and make speeches? If so, the Canadian girls, at least, would never organize.' As late as 1937, an educational manual, published by the head office of one of the garment unions, explained that, in organizing women workers, it was necessary to combat 'the idea that "it isn't nice" to even belong to a union, let alone go on the picket line.'

For some women, concerns about propriety intersected with ethnic prejudices and tensions. One Jewish woman, a labour activist in Toronto's millinery trade in the early to mid-twentieth century, recalled that many non-Jewish women millinery workers 'thought that the union was beneath them.' These Anglo-Celtic women disdained unions, apparently not only because they believed unions were not respectable but also because union membership in this case meant associating more closely with Jewish immigrants.

Were working-class women really so constrained by notions of ladylike behaviour? Their views have been hard to discover. Although there were some class variations in conceptions of femininity, it appears that restrictive, middle-class ideas of proper womanhood kept some working-class women in check. Some historians have suggested that middle-class views of women as submissive, delicate, housebound creatures were simply not applicable to the realities faced by working-class women, and therefore had little salience for them. But this claim appears to go too far. At the same time, those historians who suggest that working-class women simply absorbed all aspects of middle-class notions of proper womanhood also appear to go too far.

Restrictive notions of ladylike behaviour undoubtedly made it more difficult for some women workers to resist harsh working conditions, but overemphasizing this factor risks obscuring the major structural barriers that impeded women workers' militancy.

These debates about feminine propriety, moreover, have generally failed to consider ethnicity and race. Yet conceptions of femininity could also vary in different cultural contexts. Immigrant women from peasant backgrounds in eastern Europe may have largely dismissed Anglo-Celtic views of true womanhood, while perhaps facing other constraints that were specific to their own ethnic groups. As Mary Jary's militancy indicates, there were indeed situations where women openly defied such concerns. The immigrant Jewish community also demonstrates cultural variations in concepts of womanhood. Eastern European Jewish culture had traditionally legitimated women's gainful employment. In a context where the ideal Jewish man was a religious scholar, Jewish women were responsible for looking after the home but were not limited to that sphere. While subordinated to Jewish men, the women had a legitimate – and assertive – role to play in the marketplace, doing their share to earn a livelihood for the family. The dire poverty of so many eastern European Jews also legitimated an assertive breadwinning role for women. It is not surprising, then, that immigrant Jewish females tended to be more militant than their Anglo-Canadian or French-Canadian counterparts in the clothing industry.

More generally, women's relatively limited workplace experience restricted the possibilities of protest. Single women typically left paid labour upon marriage, and married women who went out to work tended to move in and out of the labour market, depending on the timing of pregnancies, the presence or absence of older offspring who could bring in money, and the health and employment status of their husbands or other partners. Women's household responsibilities also limited the time and energy they could put into organizing. Even single women often rushed home from work to help their mothers or do their own laundry and prepare their own meals. Unmarried women wage earners were especially burdened in cases where they had to keep house for male relatives who did not have their own wives. Few seasoned female union leaders emerged under these circumstances.

Other Barriers to Militancy

Employers were probably particularly intransigent with their female employees, who were supposed to be cheap labour, especially in highly competitive areas such as the garment industry. Moreover, employers were frequently able to pursue a 'divide and conquer' strategy by buying off male workers at the expense of the women, just as they tried to divide workers along ethnic and racial lines. It was difficult for women workers to deal with employers such as the one who treated his male workers fairly well but 'even[ed] up by taking advantage of the women.'

Joe Salsberg, an organizer for the United Cloth Hat, Cap, and Millinery Workers' International Union in the early 1920s, later recounted that, in organizing a local of female finishers, he had to work 'to overcome a silent resistance from the men' in the union. The men '*knew* that it is perhaps easier for *them* to get concessions than it will be if they become part of the union ... with the girls, with the women.' The manufacturers' threat to keep the men's wages down if they were forced to grant higher wages to the newly organized women seemed credible, particularly in view of the intense competition from unorganized Montreal firms. When the finishers did join the union, the employers were willing to grant wage increases only to the males and thus provoked strikes. The male unionists 'weren't very happy' about striking for higher wages for the finishers, declared

Salsberg, 'but they struck.' The unionists finally succeeded in winning agreements that included wage increases and union recognition for both women and men.

More broadly, there was a danger that union insistence on increased pay for female workers might lead employers to hire men instead, since much of the women's value to their employers resided in their cheap labour. Although this possibility was reduced by the sense that there were women's jobs that men could not or would not do, this job segregation was partly premised on the notion that men would not do these jobs because they paid so little. As we have seen, there were some cases, particularly during the Great Depression, where employers fired women and hired men at very low wages instead. While certain jobs were seen as natural to women and not men, this belief could sometimes be challenged.

The issue of equal pay for equal work was a particularly slippery one. On the one hand, many unions did nothing to promote equal pay, thereby failing to help women, who earned one-third to one-half less money for doing the same work as their male counterparts. On the other hand, some unions may have adopted the strategy of calling for equal pay as a way of actually trying to keep women out of particular workplaces. Although it is difficult to document deliberate motivation in such cases, we do know of a number of instances where a union's insistence on equal pay meant that women were no longer hired. This happened in Toronto's late-nineteenth-century cigar industry. Thus, supporting a union could actually work to the immediate disadvantage of women.

Another significant factor undercutting the possibilities of organization was the large number of women who lacked scarce skills and who competed for 'women's jobs' at a time when so many other jobs were deemed totally unsuitable for them. Where women did begin to organize, employers often broke their unions by firing and replacing the militants.

In numerous cases, employers defeated the strikes of those who lacked scarce skills by replacing the strikers en masse with scab labour. This was a problem that also plagued male workers lacking highly marketable skills.

Domestic servants, the largest category among women workers at the turn of the twentieth century, were particularly difficult to organize, as a result of their isolation in private homes, their unusually long and irregular hours, and their close personal relationships to their employers, especially when they boarded in their employers' homes. Some of these problems also affected other women, including homeworkers and garment workers in small, short-lived subcontractors' shops. Organizers who had to locate many scattered workers found this a much tougher task than trying to organize larger workplaces.

Many women 'voted with their feet' to protest their harsh working conditions and low pay, moving between workplaces and sectors, partly to quell the dreariness of repetitive work. In many cases, such individual transiency may have been the only available recourse, but it also undermined women's ability to organize themselves collectively.

Male Unionists' Attitudes

Men sometimes strongly supported women workers' struggles against employers. More often, however, female workers faced less than total solidarity from their 'fellow' workers and 'brother' unionists. Many male workers and male unionists were, at best, ambivalent towards women workers, and some were overtly hostile. These men thought that women did not belong in the workplace, and feared that low-wage women workers might undercut their own wages or take their jobs. Although, as we have seen, many jobs were considered unsuitable – indeed impossible – for women, there were some gray areas, particularly in the context of deskilling. The prospect of competition from women generated considerable anxiety among male workers at the time, especially because people did not know where it would all end.

Some male unionists favoured organizing blue-collar women, but many were convinced that women were too docile as a result of their allegedly inherent traits. An 1897 Ontario labour journalist stressed 'the natural timidity among women to enter into [unions].' Such stereotypes were a poor substitute for a serious analysis of the barriers that women faced. In situations where union men failed to promote women's activism, such pronouncements could become self-fulfilling prophecies.

Male unionists themselves were on the defensive, especially as firms grew in size and financial clout. Inadequate wages and the threat of unemployment (augmented by employers' use of blacklists against labour activists) were very real concerns. Employers used their power to chip away at craft skills and sometimes brought in women to do some of the newly simplified tasks. This divide-and-conquer strategy used women, as it used unskilled male immigrants, to keep workers in a competitive scramble for scarce jobs. On rare occasions, women were also brought in as strikebreakers during male workers' strikes.

Turn-of-the-century male craft unionists in particular were likely unable to appeal sincerely and effectively to women's sentiments of working-class solidarity when the men themselves had often pursued exclusionary policies. They frequently sought to exclude women from the paid labour force in general and from their own trades in particular. As the international treasurer of the American Federation of Labor (AFL) explained in 1905, 'the great principle for which we fight is opposed to taking ... the women from their homes to put them in the factory and the sweatshop.' Although there was a humanitarian side to this goal, it was distinctly paternalistic. Morever, it is difficult to ascertain whether the main issue was humanitarianism or the fear that competition from women would undermine the men's positions, for the two elements were often woven together. Thus, as a labour representative from Ontario explained in 1910, 'we think that women should not be allowed to work in the foundries, as it has a tendency to degrade them, to lower the wages of the men and to keep a number of young men out of work.'

In the late nineteenth century, such exclusionary policies had been elevated to a formal principle of the Trades and Labour Congress (TLC), which was Canada's central labour body. Its platform of principles called for the 'abolition of ... female labour in all branches of industrial life, such as mines, workshops, factories, etc.' Although this principle was changed in 1914 to a call for 'equal pay for equal work for men and women,' the TLC's antipathy towards the use of women in 'men's jobs' persisted during the First World War. As employers attacked craft workers' skills, wages, and working conditions, male unionists commonly insisted that women should be hired only when males were unavailable. These male unionists feared that wartime conditions provided employers with a golden opportunity to deskill jobs massively, lower wages, and break the backs of unions, and that the employment of women was one way to attain such goals. As one male labour activist sarcastically wrote: 'Wanted, women to take the places of men ... Sure this is a good move to reduce the wages of the men, and if they don't like it fire them – starve them to enlist [in the armed forces]. Businessmen, get wise to a good thing – this is the way to reduce your expenses, and when the men return from the war, why the game is in your hands.'

Since the wartime government refused to guarantee equal pay for women performing men's jobs while working on government contracts, male craft unionists often reacted by trying to restrict the use of female labour. At the 1918 Conference on War Problems, labour delegates tried to persuade government representatives that women should be hired only 'after full investigation had proven that all available man power had been absorbed.' They wanted women inspectors, together with 'representatives of men's organizations,' to report on 'the advisability of women undertaking any class of work (with the view of their responsibility towards the nation, as the mothers of our future citizens).'

During the First World War, support for equal pay could sometimes help underpaid women. But supporting equal pay may have been intended to remove the low-wage incentive for hiring women and thus to ensure that all available men would be hired before employers would resort to using women. Support for equal pay may also have been a way of helping to ensure that, when the war ended, women workers would be replaced by returning men. Indeed, during the war, male unionists often insisted that, in cases where women had taken over 'men's jobs,' these jobs must revert to men once the war was over. Women, they argued, should then return to the home.

In some cases, male workers were so deeply committed to the exclusion of women that they were prepared to make unusual compromises with their employers. In wartime Ontario, for example, unionized iron moulders struck to protest the hiring of women in the core room, demanding that the company install a core machine instead. Technological change was preferable, even if it threatened craft skills. Similarly, Toronto's street railway workers threatened to strike in the midst of the war if women were hired. These unionists went so far as to hint that they might accept the introduction of pay-as-you-enter cars as a better alternative to bringing in women, even though the introduction of these cars would mean the elimination of half the jobs on the street cars. In contrast, Vancouver's street railway workers' position was that they would not oppose the hiring of women as conductors as long as the women became union members and obtained equal pay.

The behaviour of many male workers was far from reflecting class solidarity, but it was not wholly indicative of a battle between the sexes either. Recognizable, common class interests could produce more ambivalence – and sometimes real solidarity. Some men began to acknowledge that the women in the labour force needed union support to improve low wages and harsh working conditions. After all, some of these female workers were their daughters, sisters, or nieces. Moreover, some men recognized that they themselves would not make gains without unionizing the women.

At the turn of the century, this ambivalence often translated into only half-hearted support for women workers' struggles. The International Brotherhood of Electrical Workers (IBEW), for example, had asserted its jurisdiction over women telephone operators but appears to have been relatively uninterested in organizing them. The executive board of the union often refused requests to help organize the operators. Although, in the period before the First World War, a few IBEW locals of women telephone operators existed in the United States, they were not given the autonomy and the voting rights normally afforded to the male locals. Skilled men in this union probably feared that if many operators were organized, the women would eventually outnumber the men and would therefore take control of the organization. The men seemed particularly to fear that unskilled operators might make poor decisions about craft issues.

The Knights of Labor, a late-nineteenth-century labour organization, was far more inclusive than the craft unions in its attempts to organize women workers. Although many Knights idealized the family wage, they strove to organize both the skilled and the unskilled, regardless of gender. Yet the organization was marked by tension between more traditional attitudes towards women and an emphasis on women's equality. On the one hand, chivalrous male Knights thought they should protect 'the fairer sex'; on the other, they welcomed women into the organization as equals. The Knights stood for equal pay for equal work and also supported women's suffrage. They argued that women workers were especially oppressed in the workplace because they could not vote. Some of the Knights' support for women's suffrage was clearly egalitarian, stressing 'the right of women to be regarded in all matters of citizenship and all relations between the government and the people as the equal of men.' At the same time, the Knights (like many middle-class social reformers) also argued that women should have the vote because their special motherly influence was needed to clean up society and protect the home. The Knights emphasized the sanctity of the working-class home and female domesticity in particular. Because they were concerned that female employees were vulnerable to the sexual advances of male supervisors, the Knights joined social reformers in pressuring the government to bring in laws against 'seduction' (what we would now call 'sexual harassment').

The Knights of Labor made impressive gains in organizing women and displayed significant male-female solidarity, as, for example, during a strike of female shoe workers in Hamilton, Ontario, in 1884. Fifty-five women struck against a wage cut, and over one hundred male shoe workers in the Knights of Labor risked their own jobs by refusing to work until the women's wage cut was rescinded. The result was a reduction in the extent of the wage cuts, and all the workers got their jobs back. Despite such actions, Leonora Barry, head of the Knights' women's department, still maintained that problems organizing women stemmed in part from the 'selfishness' of the male Knights.

After the demise of the Knights of Labor at the turn of the century, craft unions predominated for some time. The radical new Industrial Workers of the World (IWW) championed organizing both the skilled and the unskilled but actually signed up few women. Likewise, the One Big Union, founded in 1919, ambitiously proclaimed that it would organize all workers 'irrespective of nationality, sex or craft,' but, in practice, it was restricted mainly to male workers in western Canada. Although some women joined in places like Winnipeg and Vancouver, the One Big Union was largely destroyed within a couple of years, under intense opposition from employers, the state, and craft unionists.

Meanwhile, a specifically Catholic form of unionism was developing among French Canadians in Quebec. Established in 1921, the Canadian and Catholic Confederation of Labour (CCCL) brought together individual Catholic unions that had developed over the preceding decade. With Catholic chaplains acting as advisors, the CCCL was a conservative form of unionism that discouraged strikes and promoted a vision of peaceful cooperation between employees and employers. One of the main purposes of the CCCL was to try to ensure that male and female French-Canadian workers would not become involved in secular or socialist unions. As the CCCL grew in the 1920s, the 'professional associations' of employed women, which had been founded by the Fédération Nationale Saint-Jean-Baptiste, became less active. The CCCL would later become more militant, leading to a major textile strike in 1937.

In the first half of the 1930s, the Communist Party entered its most sectarian phase and launched the short-lived Workers Unity League (WUL) as a radical new trade union centre to rival the existing labour unions and organize the unorganized. In the midst of the Great Depression, the WUL tackled several sectors, from heavy industry to the textile and garment industries. In some cases the WUL focused on workers who had been ignored by the established unions (such as immigrants and women), but in other cases WUL organizing led to dual unionism and bitter fights with established unions. Such struggles often played into the hands of employers. In the garment industry, particularly in Toronto, the battle between the WUL's Industrial Union of Needle Trades Workers (IUNTW) and the TLC's International Ladies' Garment Workers' Union (ILGWU) enabled employers to play one union off against the other. The IUNTW was more effective in Winnipeg, however, and it did important organizing work among Montreal's garment workers as well. The WUL even attempted to organize waitresses, laundry workers, and clerical workers. The Communist organizers nonetheless tended to assume that women workers were of secondary importance, and they put more emphasis on organizing males in heavy industry. Moreover, neither of the rival garment unions questioned the gender division of labour, and neither did much to develop special organizing methods geared specifically to women workers.

In the late 1930s (not long after the Communist Party dissolved the WUL), the Congress of Industrial Organizations (CIO) became active in Canada. In contrast to the traditional craft unions, the CIO sought to organize skilled and unskilled blue-collar workers of both sexes, especially in mass production industries such as rubber, meat packing, and textiles. The absence of detailed studies of the CIO's efforts in Canada in this period makes it difficult to draw firm conclusions about its work with women. Despite impressive gains, CIO activists took the gender division of labour for granted in this period, and CIO contracts sometimes included unequal wage structures.

A strike at two Peterborough textile mills in 1937 sheds light on this mixed record. The CIO's United Textile Workers initially focused on organizing males at one of the mills. After three hundred workers walked off the job for better wages, union recognition, and better measures concerning piecework, the union called out the workers at a second mill owned by the same company, where many women worked. Although involved only at the last minute, many women became quite active in the strike and were among the most militant picketers, despite police intimidation. Some were recruited to join the strike committee, where they remained in the minority. One woman in particular emerged as a key strike leader, despite the fact that some people criticized her activism as unfeminine. To win public support, the union emphasized male workers' inability to be good breadwinners and made women's wages a secondary consideration. Yet the strikers refused an offer of higher wages for skilled men alone, and they held out for a month and a half. After the strike, the male-centred union did not integrate the women well, and they tended to lose interest in the organization.

Male unionists have often been reluctant to bring women into decision-making and leadership roles within the labour movement. In early-twentieth-century Vancouver, for example, Helena Gutteridge, one of the few female union leaders in British Columbia, proposed to bring together women from various unions to discuss the eight-hour day, a minimum wage for women, and mothers' allowances. The male leaders of the local trades and labour council objected, arguing that only the elected delegates could legitimately represent their unions, even in such discussions. These men decided that an existing committee of men would deal with these issues. Years later, Pearl Wedro, a Jewish immigrant active in the International Fur Workers' Union and the Communist Party in the interwar years, looked back over her life in the labour movement and concluded that 'even [in] progressive-led unions, a woman's chances are less than a man's. There's always somehow resentment to let to the very top a woman.' Despite these frustrations, she devoted her life to the labour movement. Like many other women labour organizers, who had to choose between a family and a career, she never married.

In general, the male culture of the labour movement tended to serve as a significant impediment to women's full participation in unions. At the turn of the century, if the 'real woman' belonged at home, the 'real man' belonged in the union. Skilled workers in particular tended to view manliness and notions of the inherent dignity of manhood as fundamental ideological elements in their struggle. 'Real men' were defined as those who stood shoulder to shoulder with their fellow workers, were not afraid to oppose management, and would not put up with being treated badly. Hence strikebreakers were commonly denounced as having betrayed their manhood. The sense of dignity – and indeed the conception of unionism – of many male trade unionists was bound up with their gender identity. The notion of the manly union member – indeed, the very notions of 'fraternity' and 'brotherhood' – defined women as outsiders. Although some labour organizations were less extreme in this respect than others, this masculinist emphasis remained common.

Sometimes the atmosphere of union meetings and the patterns of union socializing could also deter women. At the turn of the century, for example, the members of a Toronto labour council committee believed that women unionists did not come to the meetings because the atmosphere was 'repellent.' Many unions met in smoke-filled rooms with easy access to alcohol. As late as the interwar period, union halls were still mainly masculine territory, even where the particular union included a significant number of women.

Female Solidarity and Female Militancy

In the face of so many barriers, women workers more often relied on informal mutual assistance rather than organizing union picket lines to improve their work lives. Women working on piece rates, for example, sometimes urged the fastest workers to slow down, for they feared that management would cut their rates if too many workers were earning decent wages. A particularly fast pieceworker might even give some completed work to a slower workmate to help her make her quota. Female co-workers helped each other clean up accidental spills quickly to avoid trouble with management. Together they sometimes improvised indirect ways of subverting supervisors' orders.

At times, women were able to battle more directly for better working conditions and union rights, whether on their own, along with male co-workers, or aided by men in other trades. While women sometimes worked to build unions, more often they engaged in spontaneous strikes, without the benefits of prior unionization.

At the turn of the century, women in several cities struggled to organize themselves in a vast array of jobs – not only factory workers but also female telephone operators, retail clerks, bookbinders, laundry workers, hotel and restaurant employees, stenographers, and even domestic servants. Many of these efforts were short-lived, collapsing in the face of all the obstacles that women confronted. But the labour shortage during the First World War, combined with the upsurge in labour militancy at the war's end, reinvigorated efforts to organize a broad range of women workers, including confectionary workers, rubber workers, meat packers, retail clerks, office workers, waitresses, and domestics.

A systematic study of strikes involving women in the period from 1890 to 1920 indicates that women's militancy was significant but limited; the number of such strikes was not negligible, but it was not large either. Their strikes erupted in many sectors, including service work and public utilities. In 1907, Bell Telephone's female operators in Toronto provided a dramatic example. They faced a gruelling pace of work, serious health hazards such as electrical shocks, and low pay. At the time, management was conducting an efficiency drive and demanding a reduction in hourly pay, despite the fact that Bell's profits were increasing and the company was in a strong position as a monopoly. Without union affiliation and with little chance to plan, four hundred women operators struck. Bell brought in strikebreakers from its branches in other cities and refused to negotiate or to be bound by a royal commission established to investigate the dispute. The company argued that the women did not need better pay because they were just working for 'pin money' for a short time before marrying. Sympathetic public attention focused not on their poor wages but on concerns that the women's work at Bell was undermining their health as future mothers. As we have seen, Deputy Minister of Labour William Lyon Mackenzie King also focused on risks to the women's health and morality, when attempting to help settle the strike. Although Bell made some minor concessions, the company's powerful resources prevailed in the end. Yet these young women maintained a strong solidarity throughout the strike. Strikers who lived in families with other breadwinners, for example, gave money to those who lived alone. The militancy of the strikers was created and maintained without the benefit of strong allies or years of experience in union organizing.

Women struck most often in the garment industry and the textile industry. Most strikes in the garment industry included both women and men, and it is often not possible to ascertain what role women played on these occasions. When management of the Lowndes Company in Toronto tried to introduce a new system of speed-ups in 1905, the workers at a special shop meeting voted overwhelmingly to strike. Some women did not wait for male leadership: the next morning, three women picketers were on the scene and persuaded at least forty more people to join the walkout. Altogether, the strikers, mostly Jewish immigrants from Czarist Russia, totalled about 125 women and 75 men. The male cutters and pressers showed no interest in supporting the less skilled workers. These men continued to work, although they were reportedly just about to join the strike when the company capitulated. Two years earlier, seventy-two women at another Toronto garment shop had already shown they could act without male support. They struck to protest the price they were being charged for thread used in factory production. A committee of the women negotiated a quick settlement. In 1910, sixty women at another clothing factory obtained help from the United Garment Workers, but only after they had started a strike on their own. The early 1910s witnessed a whole series of strikes by female and male clothing workers.

Militancy in this sector continued into the interwar period. An especially important battle was the three-week strike of several thousand female dressmakers in Montreal in 1937. The official leadership of the strike was mostly male. The International Ladies' Garment Workers' Union (ILGWU) brought a female organizer, Rose Pesotta, from the United States to help with the drive. She reported that the 'pent-up resentment [of the female dressmakers] against existing conditions flared forth, and they trooped into the union office, pressing us to call strikes in their shops.' The union responded by calling everyone out. The ILGWU faced enormous opposition. In addition to the resistance from the dress manufacturers, the strikers also faced opposition from the provincial government and the Catholic unions in Quebec's clothing trades. Denouncing the ILGWU leaders as 'foreign agitators,' the Catholic unions signed a contract with the dress manufacturers just after the strike began. Catholic union leaders urged the women workers, who were mostly French Canadian, to return to work. Priests apparently joined in the denunciation of the ILGWU during their Sunday sermons, and the provincial government threatened to arrest the strike leaders. Nevertheless, most of the dressmakers joined the ILGWU's picket line, as did the skilled male dress cutters, despite their separate collective agreement with the manufacturers. Dress production ground to a halt. The employers, anxious to market their new summer dresses, finally agreed to a 10 per cent wage increase, the forty-four-hour week, union recognition, and a grievance procedure.

In the textile industry, women and men often struck together. As in the garment industry, the strikes sometimes originated among particular groups of women and expanded from there. For example, the five-week strike at the Canadian Cottons Mill in Hamilton, Ontario, in 1929 began, apparently spontaneously, when the company tried to force each female spinner to tend more machines. They refused to accept this increased workload, and the strike spread to other workers. The strike committee consisted of three women and three men, and women played an important role in sustaining the strike. The six hundred strikers engaged in mass picketing, demanding the abolition of the increased workload, the rehiring of all the workers who had lost their jobs because of the new efficiency measures, and an across-the-board 25 per cent wage increase. Confronted by a powerful employer, the workers ultimately lost the strike, but it remains an important illustration of women's militant initiatives.

Thus women in the labour force were far from completely docile. Although few historians have tried to analyse the kinds of conditions that have prompted female militancy, some tentative conclusions can be drawn from the available fragmentary evidence. Attention to this question also sheds some light on the kinds of circumstances that have led male workers and male unionists to support women workers' struggles. Like certain groups of male workers who lacked scarce skills, female workers who may have been relatively docile much of the time apparently engaged in strikes particularly during economic upturns, when there was more demand for their labour and they were therefore less vulnerable.

The tendency towards militancy was probably higher among women who had engaged in paid labour for longer intervals than usual and also among women whose skills were more highly valued. In the 1937 Peterborough textile strike, for example, the female strikers had generally been in the mills longer than their counterparts who refused to join the strike. A study of women in Quebec's textile mills indicates that the women were more militant before 1920 than in the three decades that followed, because of issues of longevity and skill. Quebec's female mill workers toiled in this industry mainly in the interval between leaving school and marrying, but this interval got shorter as the age of leaving school rose and the age of marriage fell. In addition, changes in the labour process meant that women's jobs were more crucial to the process of production in the earlier period, thereby making female militancy a little less risky.

A study that provides a detailed comparison of the textile and shoe industries in late-nineteenth-century Quebec emphasizes how important the labour process could be. In this period, women textile workers were significantly more militant than their female counterparts in the shoe industry. The subdivision of labour was less intense for female textile workers than for female shoemakers; hence the textile workers, who performed similar work, could develop a stronger sense of solidarity. In addition, the gender division of labour was more rigid in the shoe industry, and the men's and women's departments were more spatially segregated in this sector as well. As a consequence, having more in common with each other than did their counterparts in the shoe industry, male and female textile workers were more likely to develop cross-gender solidarity.

Women workers who were drawn together not only on the shop floor but also through close family and community ties were probably more inclined to develop the bonds that could lead to militancy. Similar dynamics could foster cohesiveness among male and female co-workers as well, as, for example, among Jewish immigrants in the garment industry, where close ethnic ties combined with high levels of residential and occupational concentration to heighten solidarity and militancy. Moreover, in families and close communities where females tended to work in one sector while the males worked in other sectors, the attitudes of male relatives and male friends towards unionism could have an important impact. A young woman whose father did not want her to join a strike often had trouble disobeying parental authority. On the other hand, men who were pro-union sometimes supported the militancy of women in their families and communities, especially if the employment patterns were so distinct that the men and women did not see themselves as potential competitors for jobs. After all, these men sometimes supported the militancy of their daughters, sisters, and wives because their families needed the wage increases that militancy might yield.

Ideological commitments also played a role in shaping union attitudes and actions towards women workers. The broader political climate could be important as well. In Vancouver in the 1930s, for example, depression conditions radicalized workers and drew more women workers into labour organizations and strikes than in any previous period. The political currents within particular immigrant groups were also important, as, for example, among left-wing Ukrainian, Finnish, and Jewish immigrants.

Within the working class, broad common concerns could also help overcome gender divisions as well as ethnic divisions. New work on the upsurge in labour activism at the end of the First World War highlights the unique circumstances that led to unprecedented solidarity and militancy in many parts of Canada. Most of the leaders of this revolt were Anglo-Celtic males who focused mainly on workers like themselves and often remained uneasy about women workers and male workers who were non-British immigrants. Yet despite lingering gender and ethnic divisions, women and male immigrants were drawn into the movement on an unprecedented scale. Strikes involved not only factory women (including garment, textile, shoe, and bakery and confectionery workers) but also telephone operators, female store clerks, and waitresses, in conjunction with many male strikers. In fact, a walkout by five hundred female telephone operators kicked off the Winnipeg General Strike. This heightened class solidarity and militancy stemmed from wartime discontents centring on rampant inflation, government mismanagement and corruption, business profiteering, and military conscription. Mainstream political leaders made nationalist appeals, calling on people to make great sacrifices in the fight for 'democracy,' while the government pursued anti-labour policies. Consequently, divisions among workers yielded to a stronger sense of common class grievances and class consciousness, in unprecedented ways.

Women who organized unions or went out on strike, either by themselves or together with male co-workers, fought for a variety of goals. Most often they wanted better wages, but sometimes they also fought for a shorter work week, an end to particularly onerous speed-ups, and perhaps union recognition. Their wage demands were usually structured in ways that did not disturb the significant gap between the pay for women's jobs and the pay for men's jobs. More concretely, unions often asked for a fixed across-the-board percentage increase, which actually amounted to a lower increase for lower-paid women workers. Although such militancy did not challenge the gender division of labour, it testified to the boldness with which some women struggled to improve other aspects of their work lives.

Organizations of White-Collar Workers

White-collar workers such as clerks, teachers, nurses, and social workers also formed associations and sometimes protested against such gender-based inequalities as low pay and limited career prospects, but they seldom identified with, let alone collaborated with, working-class women's campaigns. Middle-class values of propriety and respectability held greater sway among such white-collar workers than among their blue-collar counterparts. Some white-collar women workers, moreover, considered themselves socially superior to working-class women. Their class biases supplemented gender and racial ideologies in inhibiting their participation in broadly based labour protest and militancy.

Among white-collar workers, store and office clerks stood closest to blue-collar women in terms of status and earnings. Sales clerks, in particular, tended to get more help from unions than did other white-collar groups. At the same time, they generally proved much more difficult to sign up than blue-collar women. With rare exceptions, the labour movement showed little interest in organizing office clerks, who allegedly had a false sense of occupational superiority. (Indeed they would not organize in Canada until well after the Second World War.) In Quebec, the greater

success enjoyed by reformers in the Fédération Nationale
Saint-Jean-Baptiste in recruiting store and office clerks to
join their professional associations may well have had to do
with the greater respectability of these associations. As we
have seen, middle-class women formed them to prevent
secular labour unions from making inroads among French-
Canadian women workers. Although one professional association protested against a bill that would have banned
women from becoming Superior Court stenographers, these
associations emphasized social harmony and consequently
did not generally challenge the low pay or ghettoization of
their members.

Some secretaries, stenographers, clerks, bank workers,
and other white-collar workers joined Business and Professional Women's Clubs. The first such club was established
in Toronto in 1910; by 1930 seven local clubs joined to form
the Canadian Federation of Business and Professional
Women's Clubs. The clubs were generally led by women of
the liberal professions, but, as far as we can tell, most
members were low-paid, low-status clerks. Club members
seldom analysed the causes of women's subordination in
the workforce in any detail, for the members were interested primarily in promoting their own economic, social,
and educational interests. In the face of intense opposition
to female employment during the Great Depression, however, they defended even married women's entitlement to
work, as we have seen.

At times, women teachers were willing to challenge their
subordination within their profession. Protest and change
were difficult, however, precisely because gender ideology
and economic self-interest could pit male teachers against
female teachers. Many men not only accepted prevailing
gender norms, but they also feared competition from women
teachers. Consequently, although women joined teachers'
associations in various provinces, these organizations did
not act to eliminate inequalities between male and female
teachers. The Provincial Education Association of Nova

Scotia, a lobby group and scientific society for teachers, for example, recognized and accepted lower wages for women teachers by accepting lower dues from them. In its treatment of women members, moreover, the association replicated the paternalism of the surrounding society. When women prepared papers for presentation, these were presented by men as the work of anonymous 'lady teachers,' in order to protect women from having to appear on a public platform. The executive of the Nova Scotia association was all male.

But as early as 1849, an Ontario teacher complained about her own low wages and blamed her male colleagues' poor opinion of women for the low pay and status of women teachers more broadly. By the 1880s, recognition of the discrimination they faced led women teachers to begin establishing their own associations. In Quebec at the turn of the century, organizations of lay Catholic and Protestant female teachers campaigned to reduce inequities in a teachers' pension scheme that seriously disadvantaged women. By 1918 both the Federation of Women Teachers' Associations of Ontario and the Saskatoon Women's Teachers' Association demanded equal pay for equal work. The Saskatoon association also campaigned for the retention of married women teachers. Some exceptional female and male teachers actually went out on strike, notably in Moose Jaw, Saskatchewan, in 1921 and in Brandon, Manitoba, the following year. The Federation of Women Teachers' Association of Ontario contributed a significant sum to the Brandon strikers.

Nurses, too, attempted to have some say over their professional lives. The dependence of hospitals on their labour could give student trainees some leverage. In 1906, for example, nursing students at Brandon General Hospital demanded the elimination of courses in arithmetic, spelling, and composition, on the grounds that the course load was too heavy and that nurses did not need these classes. Nurses formed professional associations at the hospital, provincial, and national levels with support from other women's groups. Their associations sought legislation to make registration mandatory for graduate nurses and to prevent unqualified people from practising. Nurses also sought control over registration.

Legislators and physicians felt threatened by the prospect of nurses' having the power to regulate themselves. Some physicians feared that the prevailing health-care hierarchy would be subverted. Even without such legislation, they argued, the 'scientific training' of nurses was unfortunately replacing the gentle touch, kindly ministrations, and sympathetic interest that were intuitive, feminine attributes of nurses. The nurses' campaign was denounced as 'trade-unionism of the worst type.' Yet nurses went out on strike in Brantford, Ontario, in 1909 and in New Glasgow, Nova Scotia, in 1910.

Social workers fought against their subordination too. In 1930, for example, a Montreal social worker blamed strong prejudice against women for the appointment of relatively inexperienced men to executive positions, despite the large numbers of trained and experienced women in the field. She believed that gender stereotypes prevented men from recognizing the qualifications of their female subordinates. She complained of men who sat on the boards of social agencies but believed 'that there is nothing the family case-worker does which could not be equally well done ... by one of [their] smartest stenographers.' Other women social workers spoke up against such discrimination, expressing their concerns in professional publications, at conferences, and at meetings of social service organizations. To emphasize their qualifications and experience, they distanced themselves from unpaid volunteers, describing volunteers as 'amateurish' and 'overly sentimental.' They insisted that professional women social workers were entitled to enter into the profession's top ranks and to receive salaries equal to those paid male social workers. Ironically, their own experience of gender discrimination did not prevent female social workers from viewing the traditional family and women's traditional roles within it as central to solving many of their clients' problems.

Socialists and Feminists

The socialist movement harboured competing tendencies regarding the position of women. Some socialists found room to promote women's issues within particular branches of the left. Indeed one claimed in 1910 that 'in every department of life socialists desire the absolute equality of the sexes.' But others maintained that the left should eschew these matters. A fundamental critique of the gender division of labour in the paid labour force hardly ever emerged, even among those socialists who supported women's rights.

'Is anyone so insane as to assume that women will deliberately choose to become factory slaves, or for that matter, department store slaves rather than preside over a cosy home as a beloved wife and loving mother?' asked a socialist in 1910. Expressing traditional beliefs, he added: 'Doesn't every sensible person know that woman naturally and instinctively wants her place to be in the home?' Given the weight of custom, combined with the dismal working conditions of so many jobs and the potential satisfactions of family life, who could risk such 'insanity,' even on the left? And yet some did.

Most socialists blamed capitalists for the plight of women workers, but one uncommonly radical woman went further. 'The history of women in industry,' declared Helena Gutteridge, 'is the story of struggle against not only the capitalist class who have exploited them mercilessly, but also against the men of their own class who said because they were women they must not expect to be looked upon as co-workers or receive the same pay when doing the same kind and quantity of work.' Gutteridge criticized male workers who wanted to keep the best jobs for themselves as if these jobs belonged to them 'by divine right.' 'Why is it,' she asked, '[that] women's natural protector, "man," protects her if it is a question of his own particular welfare or comfort?' 'Thank heaven the women are awakening,' added a sanguine Gutteridge, 'and not much longer will they be exploited by employers and kicked under by their "natural protectors."'

Gutteridge herself came from an English working-class family and eventually became active in socialist and feminist campaigns in Canada, while sometimes earning her living as a garment worker. One of the few female activists on the Vancouver Trades and Labour Council, she strove to organize female laundry workers, garment workers, and domestic servants, while working for women's suffrage. Gutteridge attempted to undermine the opposition to women's paid labour by arguing that the very image of true womanhood was rooted in hypocrisy: 'Nobody ever objected to women scrubbing floors or bending over a washboard [at home]. The business of placing women on a pedestal is one of the oldest yarns I've heard. Men only object to women working when they start earning money.' Gutteridge's insistence on the dual hierarchies of class and gender was rare not only among socialists but among feminist activists as well, particularly at the turn of the century.

There were other dissident voices in the socialist camp, though few of them went as far as Gutteridge. 'The capacities of the women of today are so broadened that it is impossible to relegate them to the narrow limits of household duties and expect these to fill their lives,' argued one socialist writer. 'Under Socialism the opportunity to work will be open to every man and woman,' she declared. While they could accept the idea that single women could go out to work in a future socialist society, it was rare for turn-of-the-century socialists to argue that married women needed to be able to do so. Most socialists, like most other Canadians in this period, were convinced that married women's paid labour was bad for the family. In fact, most of these socialists blamed capitalism for driving impoverished women out to work, arguing that socialism would free women to remain in the home. One writer nonetheless expressed gratitude that marriage was no longer 'considered a woman's only salvation.' 'Woman can, and does, and will earn her own living and live her own life independent of man,' she proclaimed.

Some turn-of-the-century leftists suggested that the housewife should be relieved of drudgery through the socialization of certain aspects of housework. In a future socialist society, tasks such as cooking, sewing, and doing laundry could be taken up in collectivized settings. Those who promoted this idea were apparently a small minority within the early Canadian left, and, within this minority, some believed that the whole point of socializing housework was to enable women to devote themselves more exclusively to mothering. But others believed that socialized housework would liberate women from the confines of the home and give them more economic independence.

Many of those who manoeuvred to promote women's issues on the left assumed that because socialists were committed to freedom and equality for workers, they should be committed to freedom and equality for women as well. Yet, for a significant number of socialists, the intense focus on class oppression militated against the development of an in-depth analysis of women's oppression *as women*. From this perspective, a feminist orientation could threaten to divide the working class along gender lines, thereby weakening the class struggle, while diverting the energy of sections of the working class towards 'secondary' issues – perhaps even in alliance with bourgeois women. This point of view, taken to its logical extreme, was expressed by the Communist Party of Canada in 1931: 'The women workers have no interests apart from those of the working class generally. There is no room for "feminism" in our movement. There is only place for unity and solidarity on the basis of the joint struggle against capitalism.'

An intense focus on ethnic identity, like certain forms of

class consciousness, could also inhibit the development of feminism. Toronto's immigrant Jews, for example, forged one of the most militant and radical segments of the Canadian labour movement while fighting against anti-Semitism. For the socialists among them, their deep two-fold commitment to egalitarianism did not encompass a parallel commitment to women's rights. Jewish working-class women were less apt to form a clear critique of their position as women within the immigrant Jewish community because they shared a common sense of oppression with most of the men in this community as fellow workers and as fellow Jews. Moreover, since the family was seen as so central to the perpetuation of Jewish culture, a serious feminist challenge to the traditional norms and role structures of the Jewish family would have been seen as a dangerous cultural threat.

Meanwhile, a few non-socialist feminists called for the elimination of the gender division of labour. Emily Stowe, one of Canada's first female doctors and a strong advocate of women's rights, believed that the home was too confining for women and that each woman should be able to decide for herself what kind of work to pursue. Nellie McClung, one of Canada's most prominent suffragists, declared in 1915: 'The time will come, we hope, when women will be economically free ... when women will receive equal pay for equal work, and have all avenues of activity open to them; and ... when men will not be afraid of marriage because of the financial burden, but free men and free women will marry for love, and together work for the sustenance of their families.' Like Gutteridge, McClung pointed to the hypocrisy of those who opposed women's paid labour: 'Their offices are scrubbed by women who do their work while other people sleep – poor women who leave the sacred precincts of home to earn enough to keep the breath of life in them, who carry their scrub-pails home, through the deserted streets, long after the [street] cars have stopped running.' McClung's sympathy for the scrub women was unusual. Most feminists who boldly envisioned women's access to the professions did not concern themselves with aspects of the gender division of labour that affected less privileged female income earners.

Flora MacDonald Denison was even more radical than McClung. Born into a family that was genteel but impoverished, Denison became a dressmaker (who sometimes owned her own dress shop) and eventually a journalist. In the early twentieth century, she argued that women were imprisoned in the home: 'Too long have the four walls of a kitchen crushed the lives of the mothers of the race kept there with the idea that her duty was in the home.' Like the influential American feminist Charlotte Perkins Gilman, Denison believed that women would be emancipated only if they became economically independent of men. To free women to pursue employment, Denison declared that housework and even child care should be taken over by specially trained professionals. Beyond this, Denison maintained that 'women's sphere should only be limited by her capabilities and I believe there is no sex in the human brain.' She denounced social conventions that limited the kinds of employment that women could obtain, and she came out strongly against the gender division of labour, declaring in 1910: 'Labour is not defined by gender and washing dishes is no more feminine than the sending of a marconigram [a wireless telegram] is masculine.'

Conclusion

In the midst of the Depression, Mary Jary and her allies on the picket line fought not only for higher pay but also for human dignity. When working-class women did protest, they sometimes received significant support from the labour movement. Meanwhile, members of the 'female professions' sometimes protested against their unequal treatment within their own fields, but this did not generally lead them to consider – and fight against – gender-based discrimination in all areas of the paid labour force. Class biases were partly responsible for preventing this kind of broadly based activism. The attempts to exclude minority women from these professions suggest that ethnocentrism and racially based prejudices also impeded the development of broader activism. Although the left sometimes provided openings for addressing certain women's issues, many socialists continued to believe that women's nature was fundamentally different from men's, that women belonged in the home, and that women were unsuited for many jobs in the paid labour force. In the face of such scepticism, some radical voices were nonetheless raised to suggest different possibilities for women and work.

Conclusion

The story of Canada's women workers in the years from 1870 to 1939 is, in many ways, a grim tale. No doubt focusing on the defiant voices and the specific triumphs of employed women and their advocates would make for more inspiring reading. But such a focus would be misleading, for although women workers made some gains during this period, inequality remained deeply entrenched.

Individual women manoeuvred within serious constraints to improve their situations as much as possible. Changes that may seem small to the historian were sometimes quite important to particular individuals. A new job may have made a big difference to a young woman if, for example, it enabled her to leave behind a tyrannical supervisor or a workplace that was dimly lit and poorly ventilated. Perhaps she could then walk to work instead of having to buy street railway tickets. In addition, the many dutiful daughters who went out to work apparently felt a sense of satisfaction that they could contribute to their families' economic well-being, as did other women whose earning were so crucial to their families' survival. Women who could support themselves took pride in their ability to do so. The long-term shift away from domestic service was also a gain, since so many women saw this as one of the least desirable jobs. Yet this trend was reversed somewhat during the Great Depression. In addition, women from particularly disadvantaged ethnic and racial backgrounds continued to find that most alternatives were closed to them.

Even factory work could provide certain satisfactions. Camaraderie among co-workers may have made a difficult situation more bearable. Although women's workplace culture has seldom been investigated by Canadian historians, recent research in the United States has suggested that it may have been quite important in providing friendship and mutual assistance, fostering a sense of dignity and self-worth, and sometimes forming the basis for workplace solidarity.

Whether through their own agency, or assisted by additional forces, women occasionally did secure important improvements in wages and working conditions. At times, informal workgroup actions could subvert particularly onerous regulations or practices, for example, and some strikes were victorious. Despite all the obstacles they faced, women workers could sometimes assert themselves and win concessions, occasionally with the support of male co-workers and male unionists. Although public pressure was often ineffective in reigning in employers, at times the mobilization of public opinion helped women workers. And although laws that set minimum wages and maximum hours were generally poorly enforced, some women benefited from such legislation.

Increased access to white-collar jobs also represented an important gain for women. Many a teenage girl may have hoped that she could stay in school long enough to become a secretary instead of a factory worker. After all, office work appeared cleaner, safer, and more respectable. Yet women's access to office work in the early twentieth century was premised on major restructuring that loosely parallelled the deskilling taking place in manufacturing: key elements of office work were divided into simplified, repetitive tasks and farmed out to low-paid women who were presumed to be content with dead-end jobs. At the same time, the very respectability of many white-collar occupations was premised partly on the exclusion of women from allegedly inferior ethnic and racial groups.

Meanwhile, some women benefited by entering the professions. Although a few exceptional women managed to break into prestigious occupations such as medicine and law, many more took up the 'female professions,' including teaching and nursing. Although teachers and nurses were encased in hierarchies where their subordination was the norm, their work could nevertheless be the source of much satisfaction.

But such benefits were limited. Even as the first and second industrial revolutions ushered in many far-reaching changes, women continued to be profoundly disadvantaged. With few exceptions, women who went out to work throughout this period remained confined to low-wage female job ghettos, whether in office work, the service sector, or factories. Although a few women's jobs paid better than most, women's pay was usually low in comparison to that of men working in the same sectors. Consequently, the female garment worker, excluded from the best jobs in her factory and earning far less than male co-workers doing comparable work, had much in common with the female teacher, blocked from the more lucrative and higher-status teaching positions and earning far less than male teachers doing similar jobs.

Even the labour shortages during the First World War did not result in major changes. During the war, some women entered better-paying factory jobs in previously all-male areas – most notably in the munitions plants – but, overall, the proportion of factory workers who were female apparently increased only a little. Moreover, most women lost access to traditionally male areas of manufacturing at the war's end, particularly with the closing of the munitions plants. Although the war witnessed an increase in women's office work, this was part of a long-term trend that, while benefiting women in certain ways, also ensured that they were restricted largely to low-wage, newly routinized jobs in this sector.

Despite the major disjuncture between the image of true womanhood and the reality of increasing numbers of women going out to work, deeply rooted beliefs about woman's domestic nature persisted. These convictions appeared to legitimate women's exclusion from 'men's jobs,' as well as providing a rationale for higher pay for males, as the presumed family breadwinners. It just seemed to be 'common sense.' At the same time, women workers' experiences of dreary, repetitive jobs in the paid labour force – combined with the frequent inability to procure a living wage – reinforced the domestic ideology and the institution of marriage.

Structures of inequality remained deeply rooted throughout the period considered in these pages. Strong ideological convictions and powerful vested interests interacted to ensure women's secondary status in the world of paid labour and beyond. Whether consciously or not, employers capitalized on the ways in which the domestic ideology, ironically, provided a rationale for confining women to low-wage, dead-end jobs. After all, women were presumed to be but temporary income earners, lacking valuable skills and working only for 'pin money.' Employers in key sectors also profited from divide-and-conquer tactics, pitting male and female workers against each other, much as they pitted Anglo-Celtic workers against non-British immigrant labour. At a time when there was no comprehensive legal framework to ensure unions' collective-bargaining rights, employers' interests were commonly backed up by the police, the courts, and the government.

Meanwhile, idealized notions of true womanhood and the family wage reflected and reinforced the prerogatives of men who, after all, depended on their wives' (or other female relatives') unpaid services in the home and who commonly sought to eliminate – or at least minimize – the prospect of facing competition from females in the paid workplace. At times blue-collar males themselves felt compelled to police the boundaries of the gender division of labour to keep women out of certain areas, much as male professionals often struggled to limit women's access to their own occupations.

The efforts of middle-class social reformers on behalf of employed women were limited. Although some women's groups defended women's right to go out to work, they tended to be condescending, concerned above all to protect 'future mothers,' whom they deemed unable to protect themselves. Middle-class reformers seldom worked with the labour movement to improve the lot of women workers, and they seldom supported female strikers. They typically cared more about protecting the morality of women workers, often in controlling ways, than working to increase their wages. Class biases and racist attitudes, moreover, precluded the development of a broad sense of sisterhood. These divisions among women were compounded by distinctions between blue-collar and white-collar female workers, which prompted white-collar women to nurture a sense of superiority. The fault lines that divided them prevented women from acting collectively to overcome the disadvantages they all faced in the paid workforce.

Few fundamentally radical critiques emerged during this period. Although some socialists believed in sexual equality, they seldom articulated – or consistently fought for – goals designed specifically to reduce women's oppression. Many socialists blamed capitalism for forcing women out of their homes to work, and they believed that women would be free to remain at home in a future socialist society. Outspoken feminists who promoted women's access to the professions typically neglected to consider the impact of the gender division of labour on less-privileged women wage earners.

Towards the Twenty-First Century

The last half century has witnessed a dramatic increase in women's labour force participation rates, especially in the case of married women. This overall change is partly due to increased employer demand for female labour, particularly in white-collar jobs in the service sector. The combination of increased economic demand and demographic change has meant that married women have come to be seen as an important source of 'manpower.' During the 1950s and most of the 1960s, women tended to marry slightly earlier than in previous decades, thereby shrinking the available labour pool of single women. More importantly, fertility rates dropped sharply (despite the limited increase during the baby boom years) while life expectancy increased, so employers and government officials increasingly viewed married women as having more potential years to devote to paid labour. In addition to the decline in fertility rates, other changes in family composition have also had an impact on women's labour force participation rate. Most notably, increasing rates of divorce and separation have pushed more women to earn their own income.

As increased consumer spending came to be seen as crucial to keeping the economy moving, particularly in the aftermath of the Second World War, married women's employment could be construed as good for the economy, as it would presumably lead families to spend more on consumer goods. Indeed, increased emphasis on consumerism has pushed more women out to earn money so that they and their families could increase their purchasing power. Children have come to stay in school longer and therefore have less time to go out and work to add to their families' income. In this context, more middle-class women have been going out to work.

No longer is women's paid employment mainly an interval between school and marriage. In the 1950s, women tended to go out to work before marriage and motherhood and then return again to paid labour at middle age, once their children were grown up. More recently, even mothers of preschool children have been going out to work in increasing numbers. In fact, by the late twentieth century, far fewer women left paid labour to devote themselves exclusively to raising children, and those who did retreat from the paid labour force for this purpose were doing so for much shorter intervals. Hence families where only the husbands went out to work have become far less common. More specifically, in 1961, 65 per cent of all families corresponded to the model of the male breadwinner; by 1986, this had dropped to a mere 12 per cent.

Meanwhile, married women's labour force participation rate soared from 11 per cent in 1951 to 61 per cent in 1991 (at which point it was almost as high as the participation rate for single women). Put another way, while married women constituted 30 per cent of all women in the paid labour force in 1951, they had jumped to 64 per cent by 1991. In recent years, the patterns of women's participation in the paid labour force have been coming closer to those of men.

Throughout the twentieth century, there has thus been significant change in the number of women as a percentage of all those in the paid labour force. As we have seen, this figure climbed slowly in the first four decades of the twentieth century, from 13 per cent in 1901 to 17 per cent in 1931 and almost 20 per cent in 1941. More dramatic changes have taken place in the last half century, from 22 per cent in 1951 to 34 per cent in 1971 and almost 45 per cent in 1991.

In this context, the debates concerning women's paid labour that took place in the period from 1870 to 1939 have taken on new dimensions in the last sixty-five years. Women's growing importance in the paid labour force was more apparent during the Second World War (1939–45) than during the First World War and became even more so in the last half of the twentieth century. The increased economic significance of women's paid labour led to reduced discrimination against married women but not automatically to widespread improvements for employed women. Nonetheless, the disjuncture between the domestic ideology and the reality of women workers became more dramatic, particularly as more and more married women went out to work. This trend led to more extensive questioning of gender roles. More women began to protest their secondary status in the paid labour force, and they were sometimes joined by male allies. Because the economy had come to rely so heavily on women's labour as well as men's, women's protests eventually had to be taken more seriously, although there were still limits to what could be accomplished.

Significant protest developed even before the emergence of the second wave of the women's movement in the mid-to-late 1960s. In the aftermath of the Second World War, some individuals and groups struggled to reduce the inequality that employed women encountered. These activists were often loosely linked to the human rights campaigns that developed in the aftermath of the war. Many of the key human rights initiatives took place in Ontario. In the late 1940s, activists in Ontario focused especially on pushing for legislation that would prohibit discrimination in employment on the basis of 'race, creed, colour, nationality, ancestry or place of origin.' The Business and Professional Women's Clubs of Ontario, together with the Toronto branch of the National Council of Women, called for the inclusion of sex as one of the prohibited grounds of discrimination, as did Ontario MPP Agnes Macphail. But, at that time, most human rights activists held fast to conventional beliefs about women's fundamental nature, and, with few exceptions, they were therefore blind to much of the discrimination women faced. When Ontario's Fair Employment Practices Act became law in 1951, it did not include sex discrimination. Nor did the Ontario Human Rights Code, which was enacted in 1962.

The more specific demand for equal pay for equal work had become important during and immediately after the Second World War. Although some supporters of equal pay legislation hoped that it would motivate employers to switch to male workers (especially at the war's end), some women's groups were pushing hard for equal pay as a human rights issue. As with the Fair Employment Practices Act, Ontario pioneered the way, passing the Female Employees Fair Remuneration Act in 1951. But the act was severely limited in scope: it applied only to a woman who was doing the exact same job as a man in the same workplace. Minute differences in the man's and woman's jobs enabled the employer to circumvent the law. In addition, the comparable man and woman had to be working under the same roof rather than in different branches of the same firm. Groups such as the Co-operative Commonwealth Federation (CCF), the Business and Professional Women's Clubs, and the YWCA pressed for a broader law that would ensure equal pay for men and women doing comparable work.

By the 1950s, key employers and policy makers had come to realize that women (particularly married women) were becoming a more crucial source of labour power. This growing awareness of the increasing need for women's labour led to the removal of some discriminatory practices, including the federal government's elimination, in 1955, of the prohibition against married women working in the federal civil service. Employers in the private sector also became increasingly willing to lift the marriage bar. A number of government women's bureaus were established – at the federal level in 1953 and in Ontario in 1963, for example. Although the establishment of these bureaus was partly a response to pressure from women's groups, the main motivation apparently stemmed from the economic need to 'facilitate the integration of women into the labour force.' The women who ran these bureaus became leading advocates of a range of measures designed to promote women's equality in the paid labour force, such as better training and vocational opportunities for women, provisions for maternity leave, and access to child care. Among other things, the Ontario Women's Bureau pushed for anti-discrimination legislation, leading to the province's Women's Equal Employment Opportunity Act in 1970. Two years later, the Ontario Human Rights Code was finally amended to prohibit sex discrimination. Meanwhile, at the federal level, the Canadian Bill of Rights had been enacted in 1960, with sex included as one of the prohibited grounds of discrimination.

The resurgence of the women's movement in the mid-to-late 1960s pushed women's rights much more to the forefront of public attention, especially with the establishment of the Royal Commission on the Status of Women, which held hearings in the late 1960s and issued its report in 1970. Feminist groups pushed for equal pay for work of equal value. They also pressed hard for women's access to all kinds of jobs, ranging from high-level management positions to heavy blue-collar work (such as the 'Women into Stelco' campaign in Hamilton, Ontario, in 1980). The National Action Committee on the Status of Women (NAC), founded in the early 1970s, has played a key role in pushing for employment equity measures as well as a wide range of other feminist causes. Fairly broad pay-equity measures were finally enacted in most Canadian jurisdictions by the late 1970s and were then shaped into more proactive forms in some jurisdictions in the 1980s and 1990s. By the end of the twentieth century, measures had been enacted to promote employment equity, particularly at the federal level, but these provisions have major weaknesses, including serious problems of enforcement.

In pressing for measures such as pay equity and maternity leave, women's groups have received increasing support from the labour movement. With the emergence of large unions in the public sector in the 1960s and 1970s, many more women have become union members, and there has also been an increase in women's participation in leadership positions in the labour movement. Although unions could become more responsive to women's concerns, the late twentieth century witnessed important change in this regard. But as the century drew to a close, the labour movement itself has been weakened by intransigent employers and unsympathetic, neo-conservative governments.

Despite the various achievements of feminist groups and

their allies, and despite the dramatic increase in women's labour force participation rates in the last half of the twentieth century, some aspects of women's paid employment have scarcely changed. At the dawn of the twenty-first century, the sharp wage gap between male and female earners continues. This is partly due to the fact that more women than men opt for part-time work, for women continue to bear most of the responsibility for housework and childrearing, in a society with an acute scarcity of child-care centres. But as we have seen, even full-time women workers earn just 71 per cent of their male counterparts' earnings. In addition, although women were entering a wider range of occupations by the late twentieth century, most women continue to be confined to low-wage female job ghettos (especially in clerical work), consisting of tedious, repetitive jobs with little prospect of advancement. Women of colour have been especially disadvantaged. By and large, they have been restricted to the most menial, poorly paid jobs within female job ghettos.

Genuine equality would mean more than men and women just taking equal shares of the bad jobs and the good jobs. The quest for social justice requires examining how the hierarchies of gender, class, and ethnicity and race have interacted to reinforce multiple inequalities. These divisive dynamics have enabled some to feel marginally better off than others while enabling a few to profit immensely. In the face of dwindling natural resources and increasing social and economic disparities, it is more important than ever to understand these dynamics and forge multifaceted human rights alliances.

Bibliography

Introduction

Acheson, Thomas William. *Saint John: The Making of a Colonial Urban Community.* Toronto: University of Toronto Press, 1985.

Anderson, Karen. *Chain Her by One Foot: The Subjugation of Native Women in Seventeenth-Century New France.* New York: Routledge, 1991.

Backhouse, Constance. *Colour-Coded: A Legal History of Racism in Canada, 1900–1950.* Toronto: University of Toronto Press, 1999.

Bittermann, Rusty. 'Women and the Escheat Movement: The Politics of Everyday Life on Prince Edward Island.' In *Rethinking Canada: The Promise of Women's History.* 3rd ed. Ed. Veronica Strong-Boag and Anita Clair Fellman, 79–92. Toronto: Oxford University Press, 1997.

Bouchard, Gerard. 'Through the Meshes of Patriarchy: The Male/Female Relationship in Saguenay Peasant Society, 1860–1930.' *History of the Family* 4, no. 4 (1999): 397–425.

Christie, Nancy. 'By Necessity or by Right: The Language and Experience of Gender at Work.' *Labour/Le Travail* 50 (Fall 2002): 117–48.

Cohen, Marjorie Griffin. *Women's Work, Markets, and Economic Development in Nineteenth-Century Ontario.* Toronto: University of Toronto Press, 1988.

Comacchio, Cynthia R. *The Infinite Bonds of Family: Domesticity in*

Canada, 1850–1940. Toronto: University of Toronto Press, 1999.

Cook, Ramsay, and Wendy Mitchinson, eds. *The Proper Sphere: Woman's Place in Canadian Society*. Toronto: Oxford University Press, 1976.

Crowley, Terry. 'Rural Labour.' In *Labouring Lives: Work and Workers in Nineteenth-Century Ontario*, ed. Paul Craven, 13–105. Toronto: University of Toronto Press, 1995.

Devens, Carol. 'Separate Confrontations: Gender as a Factor in Indian Adaptation to European Colonization in New France.' In *Rethinking Canada: The Promise of Women's History*. 3rd ed. Ed. Veronica Strong-Boag and Anita Clair Fellman, 11–32. Toronto: Oxford University Press, 1997.

Errington, Jane. *Wives and Mothers, Schoolmistresses and Scullery Maids: Working Women in Upper Canada, 1790–1840*. Montreal: McGill-Queen's University Press, 1995.

Frager, Ruth A. 'Labour History and the Interlocking Hierarchies of Class, Ethnicity, and Gender: A Canadian Perspective.' *International Review of Social History* 44 (1999): 217–47.

Greer, Allan. *Peasant, Lord, and Merchant: Rural Society in Three Quebec Parishes, 1740–1840*. Toronto: University of Toronto Press, 1985.

Hewitt, Nancy A. 'Beyond the Search for Sisterhood: American Women's History in the 1990s.' In *Unequal Sisters: A Multicultural Reader in U.S. Women's History*, ed. Vicki L. Ruiz and Ellen Carol DuBois, 1–20. New York: Routledge, 2000.

Iacovetta, Franca. 'Manly Militants, Cohesive Communities, and Defiant Domestics.' *Labour/Le Travail* 36 (Fall 1995): 217–52.

Pierson, Ruth Roach. 'Experience, Difference, Dominance and Voice in the Writing of Canadian Women's History.' In *Writing Women's History: International Perspectives*, ed. Karen Offen, Ruth Roach Pierson, and Jane Rendall, 79–106. Bloomington: Indiana University Press, 1991.

Prentice, Alison, Paula Bourne, Gail Cuthbert Brandt, Beth Light, Wendy Mitchinson, Naomi Black. *Canadian Women: A History*. 2nd ed. Toronto: Harcourt Brace, 1996.

Sangster, Joan. 'Feminism and the Making of Canadian

Working-Class History: Exploring the Past, Present and Future.'
Labour/Le Travail 46 (Fall 2000): 127–65.

Scott, Joan. W. 'The Woman Worker.' In *A History of Women in the West.* Volume 4. *Emerging Feminism from Revolution to World War,* ed. Geneviève Fraisse and Michelle Perrot, 399–426. Cambridge: Harvard University Press, 1993.

Shoemaker, Nancy, ed. *Negotiators of Change: Historical Perspectives on Native American Women.* New York: Routledge, 1995.

Walker, James W.St.G. *'Race,' Rights and the Law in the Supreme Court of Canada.* Waterloo, ON: Osgoode Society for Canadian Legal History, 1997.

Chapter 1 Industrial Capitalism and Women's Work

Abella, Irving, and David Millar, eds. *The Canadian Worker in the Twentieth Century.* Toronto: Oxford University Press, 1978.

Adilman, Tamara. 'A Preliminary Sketch of Chinese Women and Work in British Columbia, 1858–1950.' In *Not Just Pin Money,* ed. Barbara K. Latham and Roberta J. Pazdro, 53–78. Victoria: Camosun College, 1984.

Avery, Donald H. *Reluctant Host: Canada's Response to Immigrant Workers, 1896–1994.* Toronto: McClelland and Stewart, 1995.

Backhouse, Constance B. 'Nineteenth-Century Canadian Prostitution Law: Reflection of a Discriminatory Society.' *Histoire sociale/Social History* 18, no. 36 (1985): 387–423.

Barber, Marilyn. *Immigrant Domestic Servants in Canada.* Ottawa: Canadian Historical Association, 1991.

Bradbury, Bettina. *Working Families: Age, Gender, and Daily Survival in Industrializing Montreal.* Toronto: McClelland and Stewart, 1993.

Brand, Dionne, ed. *No Burden to Carry: Narratives of Black Working Women in Ontario, 1920s to 1950s.* Toronto: Women's Press, 1991.

Brand, Dionne. '"We weren't allowed to go into factory work until Hitler started the war": The 1920s to the 1940s.' In Peggy Bristow, Dionne Brand, Linda Carty, Afua P. Cooper, Sylvia Hamilton, and Adrienne Shadd, *'We're Rooted Here and They*

Can't Pull Us Up': Essays in African Canadian Women's History,
171–91. Toronto: University of Toronto Press, 1994.

Brandt, Gail Cuthbert. 'The Transformation of Women's Work
in the Quebec Cotton Industry, 1920–1950.' In *The Character of
Class Struggle: Essays in Canadian Working-Class History, 1850–
1985,* ed. Bryan D. Palmer, 115–34. Toronto: McClelland and
Stewart, 1986.

– '"Weaving It Together": Life Cycle and the Industrial Experience of Female Cotton Workers in Quebec, 1910–1950.' In
The Neglected Majority: Essays in Canadian Women's History.
Volume 2. Ed. Alison Prentice and Susan Mann Trofimenkoff,
160–73. Toronto: McClelland and Stewart, 1985.

Burgess, Joanne. 'L'Industrie de la chaussure à Montréal, 1840–
1870: Le passage de l'artisanat à la fabrique.' *La Revue de
l'histoire de l'Amérique française* 31, no. 2 (1977): 187–210.

Burr, Christina. 'Defending "The Arts Preservative": Class and
Gender Relations in the Printing Trades Union, 1850–1914.'
Labour/Le Travail 31 (Spring 1993): 47–75.

Cockburn, Cynthia. *Brothers: Male Dominance and Technological
Change.* London: Pluto Press, 1983.

Connelly, Patricia. *Last Hired, First Fired: Women and the Canadian
Work Force.* Toronto: Women's Press, 1978.

Copp, Terry. *The Anatomy of Poverty: The Condition of the Working
Class in Montreal, 1897–1929.* Toronto: McClelland and
Stewart, 1974.

Fahrni, Magda. '"Ruffled" Mistresses and "Discontented" Maids:
Respectability and the Case of Domestic Service, 1880–1914.'
Labour/Le Travail 39 (Spring 1997): 69–97.

Ferland, Jacques. '"In Search of the Unbound Prometheia": A
Comparative View of Women's Activism in Two Quebec Industries, 1869–1908.' *Labour/Le Travail* 24 (Fall 1989): 11–45.

Forestell, Nancy M. 'Times Were Hard: The Pattern of Women's
Paid Labour in St John's between the Two World Wars.'
Labour/Le Travail 24 (Fall 1989): 147–66.

Frager, Ruth A. *Sweatshop Strife: Class, Ethnicity, and Gender in the
Jewish Labour Movement of Toronto, 1900–1939.* Toronto: University of Toronto Press, 1992.

Heron, Craig. *The Canadian Labour Movement: A Short History.* Toronto: Lorimer, 1996.

– 'Factory Workers.' In *Labouring Lives: Work and Workers in Nineteenth-Century Ontario,* ed. Paul Craven, 479–590. Toronto: University of Toronto Press, 1995.

Hinther, Rhonda L. 'The Oldest Profession in Winnipeg: The Culture of Prostitution in the Point Douglas Segregated District, 1909–1912.' *Manitoba History* 41 (Spring/Summer 2001): 2–13.

Hurl, Lorna F. 'Overcoming the Inevitable: Restricting Child Factory Labour in Late Nineteenth Century Ontario.' *Labour/ Le Travail* 21 (Spring 1988): 87–123.

Kinnear, Mary. *A Female Economy: Women's Work in a Prairie Province, 1870–1970.* Montreal: McGill-Queen's University Press, 1998.

Kealey, Gregory S. *Toronto Workers Respond to Industrial Capitalism, 1867–1892.* Toronto: University of Toronto Press, 1980.

Kessler-Harris, Alice. *Out to Work: A History of Wage-Earning Women in the United States.* New York: Oxford University Press, 1982.

Kobayashi, Audrey. 'For the Sake of the Children: Japanese/ Canadian Workers/Mothers.' In *Women, Work, and Place,* ed. Audrey Kobayashi, 45–73. Montreal: McGill-Queen's University Press, 1994.

Lacelle, Claudette. *Urban Domestic Servants in 19th-Century Canada.* Ottawa: Environment Canada, 1987.

Lavigne, Marie, and Jennifer Stoddart. 'Ouvrières et travailleuses montréalaises, 1900–1940.' In *Travailleuses et féministes: Les Femmes dans la société québécoise,* ed. Marie Lavigne and Yolande Pinard, 99–113. Montreal: Boréal Express, 1983.

Leslie, Genevieve. 'Domestic Service in Canada, 1880–1920.' In *Women at Work: Ontario, 1850–1930,* ed. Janice Acton, Penny Goldsmith, and Bonnie Shepard, 71–125. Toronto: Canadian Women's Educational Press, 1974.

Leacy, F.H., ed. *Historical Statistics of Canada.* Ottawa: Statistics Canada, 1983.

Light, Beth, and Ruth Roach Pierson, eds. *No Easy Road: Women in Canada, 1920s to 1960s.* Toronto: New Hogtown Press, 1990.

Lindström-Best, Varpu. *Defiant Sisters: A Social History of Finnish Immigrant Women in Canada.* Toronto: Multicultural History Society of Ontario, 1988.

McCallum, Margaret E. 'Separate Spheres: The Organization of Work in a Confectionery Factory – Ganong Bros., St Stephen, New Brunswick.' *Labour/Le Travail* 24 (Fall 1989): 69–91.

McIntosh, Robert. 'Sweated Labour: Female Needleworkers in Industrializing Canada.' *Labour/Le Travail* 32 (Fall 1993): 105–39.

Morin, Albanie. 'Les Femmes dans la lutte syndicale au Québec (industrie du textile-cotton).' *L'égale* 1 (1976): 17–22.

Morton, Suzanne. *Ideal Surroundings: Domestic Life in a Working-Class Suburb in the 1920s.* Toronto: University of Toronto Press, 1995.

– 'Separate Spheres in a Separate World: African–Nova Scotian Women in Late-19th-Century Halifax County.' In *Separate Spheres: Women's Worlds in the 19th-Century Maritimes,* ed. Janet Guildford and Suzanne Morton, 185–211. Fredericton: Acadiensis Press, 1994.

Muise, D.A. 'The Industrial Context of Inequality: Female Participation in Nova Scotia's Paid Labour Force, 1871–1921.' *Acadiensis* 20, no. 2 (1991): 3–31.

Muszynski, Alicja. *Cheap Wage Labour: Race and Gender in the Fisheries of British Columbia.* Montreal: McGill-Queen's University Press, 1996.

Myers, Sharon. '"Not to Be Ranked as Women": Female Industrial Workers in Turn-of-the-Century Halifax.' In *Separate Spheres: Women's Worlds in the 19th-Century Maritimes,* ed. Janet Guildford and Suzanne Morton, 161–85. Fredericton: Acadiensis Press, 1994.

Newton, Janice. 'From Wage Slave to White Slave: The Prostitution Controversy and the Early Canadian Left.' In *Beyond the Vote: Canadian Women and Politics,* ed. Linda Kealey and Joan Sangster, 217–36. Toronto: University of Toronto Press, 1989.

Norrie, Kenneth, and Douglas Owram. *A History of the Canadian Economy.* Toronto: Harcourt Brace Jovanovich, 1991.

Palmer, Bryan D. *A Culture in Conflict: Skilled Workers and Indus-*

trial Capitalism in Hamilton, Ontario, 1860–1914. Montreal: McGill-Queen's University Press, 1979.

Palmer, Howard. 'Reluctant Hosts: Anglo-Canadian Views of Multiculturalism in the Twentieth Century.' In *Immigration in Canada: Historical Perspectives,* ed. Gerald Tulchinsky, 297–333. Toronto: Copp Clark Longman, 1994.

Parr, Joy. *The Gender of Breadwinners: Women, Men, and Change in Two Industrial Towns, 1880–1950.* Toronto: University of Toronto Press, 1990.

Patrias, Carmela. *Patriots and Proletarians: Politicizing Hungarian Immigrants in Interwar Canada.* Montreal: McGill-Queen's University Press, 1994.

Piva, Michael J. *The Condition of the Working Class in Toronto, 1900–1921.* Ottawa: University of Ottawa Press, 1979.

Roberts, Wayne. *Honest Womanhood: Feminism, Femininity and Class Consciousness among Toronto Working Women, 1893 to 1914.* Toronto: New Hogtown Press, 1976.

Rotenberg, Lori. 'The Wayward Worker: Toronto's Prostitute at the Turn of the Century.' In *Women at Work: Ontario, 1850–1930,* ed. Janice Acton, Penny Goldsmith, and Bonnie Shepard, 33–69. Toronto: Canadian Women's Educational Press, 1974.

Ryley, Bay. *Gold Diggers of the Klondike: Prostitution in Dawson City, Yukon, 1898–1908.* N.p.: Watson and Dwyer, 1997.

Sangster, Joan. *Earning Respect: The Lives of Working Women in Small-Town Ontario, 1920–1960.* Toronto: University of Toronto Press, 1995.

Smillie, Christine. 'The Invisible Workforce: Women Workers in Saskatchewan from 1905 to World War II.' *Saskatchewan History* 39, no. 2 (1986): 62–79.

Steedman, Mercedes. *Angels of the Workplace: Women and the Construction of Gender Relations in the Canadian Clothing Industry, 1890–1940.* Toronto: Oxford University Press, 1997.

Strong-Boag, Veronica. *The New Day Recalled: Lives of Girls and Women in English Canada, 1919–1939.* Toronto: Copp Clark Pitman, 1988.

Swyripa, Frances. *Wedded to the Cause: Ukrainian-Canadian Women and Ethnic Identity, 1891–1991.* Toronto: University of Toronto Press, 1993.

Tillotson, Shirley. '"We May All Soon Be 'First-Class Men'"': Gender and Skill in Canada's Early Twentieth Century Urban Telegraph Industry.' *Labour/Le Travail* 27 (Spring 1991): 97–125.

Urquhart, M.C., and K.A.H. Buckley, eds. *Historical Statistics of Canada.* Toronto: Macmillan, 1965.

Whitaker, Reg. *Canadian Immigration Policy since Confederation.* Ottawa: Canadian Historical Association, 1991.

Women's Book Committee, Chinese National Council. *Jin Guo: Voices of Chinese Canadian Women.* Toronto: Women's Press, 1992.

Chapter 2   White Collars

Axelrod, Paul. *The Promise of Schooling: Education in Canada, 1800–1914.* Toronto: University of Toronto Press, 1997.

Barman, Jean, Neil Sutherland, and J. Donald Wilson, eds. *Children, Teachers and Schools in the History of British Columbia.* Calgary: Detselig, 1995.

Brand, Dionne, ed. *No Burden to Carry: Narratives of Black Working Women in Ontario, 1920s to 1950s.* Toronto: Women's Press, 1991.

Coburn, Judi. '"I See and Am Silent": A Short History of Nursing in Ontario.' In *Women at Work: Ontario, 1850–1930,* ed. Janice Acton, Penny Goldsmith, and Bonnie Shepard, 127–63. Toronto: Canadian Women's Educational Press, 1974.

Connelly, Patricia. *Last Hired, First Fired: Women and the Canadian Work Force.* Toronto: Women's Press, 1978.

Danylewycz, Marta. *Taking the Veil: An Alternative to Marriage, Motherhood, and Spinsterhood in Quebec, 1840–1920.* Toronto: McClelland and Stewart, 1987.

Graham, Elizabeth. 'Schoolmarms and Early Teaching in Ontario.' In *Women at Work: Ontario, 1850–1930,* ed. Janice Acton, Penny Goldsmith, and Bonnie Shepard, 165–209. Toronto: Canadian Women's Educational Press, 1974.

Guildford, Janet. '"Separate Spheres": The Feminization of Public School Teaching in Nova Scotia, 1838–1880.' In *Separate Spheres: Women's Worlds in the 19th-Century Maritimes*, ed. Janet Guildford and Suzanne Morton, 119–45. Fredericton: Acadiensis Press, 1994.

Holowach-Amiot, Elaine. 'Assimilation or Preservation: Ukrainian Teachers in Saskatchewan, 1905–20.' MA thesis, McGill University, 1985.

Kessler-Harris, Alice. *Out to Work: A History of Wage-Earning Women in the United States*. New York: Oxford University Press, 1982.

Kinnear, Mary. *A Female Economy: Women's Work in a Prairie Province, 1870–1970*. Montreal: McGill-Queen's University Press, 1998.

– *In Subordination: Professional Women, 1870–1970*. Montreal: McGill-Queen's University Press, 1995.

Knox, Ellen M. *The Girl of the New Day*. Toronto: McClelland and Stewart, 1919.

Leacy, F.H., ed. *Historical Statistics of Canada*. Ottawa: Statistics Canada, 1983.

Lowe, Graham S. *Women in the Administrative Revolution*. Toronto: University of Toronto Press, 1987.

Light, Beth, and Ruth Roach Pierson, eds. *No Easy Road: Women in Canada, 1920s to 1960s*. Toronto: New Hogtown Press, 1990.

McPherson, Kathryn. *Bedside Matters: The Transformation of Canadian Nursing, 1900–1990*. Toronto: Oxford University Press, 1996.

Monod, David. *Store Wars: Shopkeepers and the Culture of Mass Marketing, 1890–1939*. Toronto: University of Toronto Press, 1996.

Munro, Alice. *The Love of a Good Woman*. Toronto: McClelland and Stewart, 1998.

Prentice, Alison. 'The Feminization of Teaching.' In *The Neglected Majority: Essays in Canadian Women's History*, ed. Susan Mann Trofimenkoff and Alison Prentice, 49–65. Toronto: McClelland and Stewart, 1977.

Prentice, Alison, and Susan Houston. *Schooling and Scholars in*

Nineteenth-Century Ontario. Toronto: University of Toronto
Press, 1988.

Reynolds, Cecilia, and Harry Smaller. 'Ontario School Teachers:
A Gendered View of the 1930s.' *Historical Studies in Education* 6
(1994): 151–69.

Roberts, Wayne. *Honest Womanhood: Feminism, Femininity and
Class Consciousness among Toronto Working Women, 1893 to 1914.*
Toronto: New Hogtown Press, 1976.

Strong-Boag, Veronica. *The New Day Recalled: Lives of Girls and
Women in English Canada, 1919–1939.* Toronto: Copp Clark
Pitman, 1988.

Struthers, James. '"Lord Give Us Men": Women and Social Work
in English Canada, 1918–1953.' Canadian Historical Association *Historical Papers* (1983): 96–112.

Struthers, James. 'A Profession in Crisis: Charlotte Whitton and
Canadian Social Work in the 1930s.' In *The Depression in
Canada: Responses to Economic Crisis,* ed. Michiel Horn, 229–45.
Toronto: Copp Clark Pitman, 1988.

Urquhart, M.C., and K.A.H. Buckley, eds. *Historical Statistics of
Canada.* Toronto: Macmillan, 1965.

Chapter 3   In Times of Crisis

Abella, Irving, and David Millar, eds. *The Canadian Worker in the
Twentieth Century.* Toronto: Oxford University Press, 1978.

Baillargeon, Denyse. *Making Do: Women, Family and Home in
Montreal during the Great Depression.* Waterloo, ON: Wilfrid
Laurier University Press, 1999.

Grayson, L.M., and Michael Bliss, eds. *The Wretched of Canada:
Letters to R.B. Bennett, 1930–1935.* Toronto: University of
Toronto Press, 1971.

Hobbs, Margaret. 'Gendering Work and Welfare: Women's
Relationship to Wage-Work and Social Policy in Canada
during the Great Depression.' PhD diss., University of
Toronto, 1995.

Hobbs, Margaret. 'Equality and Difference: Feminism and the
Defence of Women Workers During the Great Depression.'
Labour/Le Travail 32 (Fall 1993): 201–23.

Horn, Michiel. 'Introduction.' In *The Depression in Canada: Responses to Economic Crisis*, ed. Michiel Horn, 1–12. Toronto: Copp Clark Pitman, 1988.

Kealey, Linda. *Enlisting Women for the Cause: Women, Labour, and the Left in Canada, 1890–1920*. Toronto: University of Toronto Press, 1998.

Lutz, John. 'Gender and Work in Lekwammen Families, 1843–1970.' In *Gendered Pasts: Historical Essays in Femininity and Masculinity in Canada*, ed. Kathryn McPherson, Cecilia Morgan, and Nancy M. Forestell, 80–106. Toronto: Oxford University Press, 1999.

Pierson, Ruth Roach. 'Gender and the Unemployment Insurance Debates in Canada, 1934–1940.' *Labour/Le Travail* 25 (Spring 1990): 77–103.

Powell, Mary Patricia. 'A Response to the Depression: The Local Council of Women of Vancouver.' In *The Depression in Canada: Responses to Economic Crisis*, ed. Michiel Horn, 12–30. Toronto: Copp Clark Pitman, 1988.

Ramkhalawansingh, Ceta. 'Women during the Great War.' In *Women at Work: Ontario, 1850–1930*, ed. Janice Acton, Penny Goldsmith, and Bonnie Shepard, 261–307. Toronto: Canadian Women's Educational Press, 1974.

Street, Kori. 'Bankers and Bomb Makers: Gender Ideology and Women's Paid Work in Banking and Munitions during the First World War in Canada.' PhD diss., University of Victoria, 2001.

Chapter 4   Social Reform and Regulation

Backhouse, Constance. *Petticoats and Prejudice: Women and Law in Nineteenth-Century Canada*. Toronto: Women's Press, 1991.

Canada Investigates Industrialism: The Royal Commission on the Relations of Labor and Capital, 1889. Edited by Gregory Kealey. Toronto: University of Toronto Press, 1973.

Chown, Alice A. *The Stairway*. Toronto: University of Toronto Press, 1988 (originally published in 1921).

Christie, Nancy. *Engendering the State: Family, Work, and Welfare in Canada*. Toronto: University of Toronto Press, 2000.

Cook, Ramsay. *The Regenerators: Social Criticism in Late Victorian English Canada.* Toronto: University of Toronto Press, 1985.

Frager, Ruth A. 'Class, Ethnicity, and Gender in the Eaton Strikes of 1912 and 1934.' In *Gender Conflicts: New Essays in Women's History*, ed. Franca Iacovetta and Mariana Valverde, 189–228. Toronto: University of Toronto Press, 1992.

Guest, Dennis. *The Emergence of Social Security in Canada.* Vancouver: University of British Columbia Press, 1980.

Hébert, Karine. 'A Maternalist Organization in Quebec: The Fédération Nationale Saint-Jean-Baptiste and the Struggle for Women's Suffrage.' In *Quebec since 1800: Selected Readings*, ed. Michael D. Behiels, 469–92. Toronto: Irwin, 2002.

Hobbs, Margaret. '"Dead Horses" and "Muffled Voices": Protective Legislation, Education and Minimum Wage for Women in Ontario.' MA thesis, University of Toronto, 1985.

Kinnear, Mary. *A Female Economy: Women's Work in a Prairie Province, 1870–1970.* Montreal: McGill-Queen's University Press, 1998.

Klein, Alice, and Wayne Roberts. 'Besieged Innocence: The "Problem" and Problems of Working Women, Toronto, 1896–1914.' In *Women at Work: Ontario, 1850–1930*, ed. Janice Acton, Penny Goldsmith, and Bonnie Shepard, 211–59. Toronto: Canadian Women's Educational Press, 1974.

Lavigne, Marie, Yolande Pinard, and Jennifer Stoddart. 'The Fédération Nationale Saint-Jean-Baptiste and the Women's Movement in Quebec.' In *A Not Unreasonable Claim: Women and Reform in Canada, 1880s-1920s*, ed. Linda Kealey, 71–87. Toronto: Women's Press, 1979.

Leroux, Éric. 'Un Moindre mal pour les travailleuses? La Commission du salaire minimum des femmes du Québec, 1925–1937.' *Labour/Le Travail* 51 (Spring 2003): 81–114.

Little, Margaret. *No Car, No Radio, No Liquor Permit: The Moral Regulation of Single Mothers in Ontario, 1920–1997.* Toronto: Oxford University Press, 1998.

Machar, Agnes Maule. *Roland Graeme: Knight. A Novel of Our Time.* Toronto: W. Briggs, 1906.

McCallum, Margaret E. 'Keeping Women in Their Place: The Minimum Wage in Canada, 1910–25.' *Labour/Le Travail* 17 (Spring 1986): 29–56.

Mitchinson, Wendy. 'The WCTU: "For God, Home and Native Land" – A Study in Nineteenth-Century Feminism.' In *A Not Unreasonable Claim: Women and Reform in Canada, 1880s-1920s*, ed. Linda Kealey, 151–67. Toronto: Women's Press, 1979.

Russell, Bob. 'A Fair or a Minimum Wage? Women Workers, the State, and the Origins of Wage Regulation in Western Canada.' *Labour/Le Travail* 28 (Fall 1991): 59–88.

Sangster, Joan. 'The 1907 Bell Telephone Strike: Organizing Women Workers.' *Labour/Le Travailleur* 3 (1978): 109–30.

– 'The Softball Solution: Female Workers, Male Managers and the Operation of Paternalism at Westclox, 1923–60.' *Labour/Le Travail* 32 (Fall 1993): 167–99.

Strange, Carolyn. *Toronto's Girl Problem: The Perils and Pleasures of the City, 1880–1930*. Toronto: University of Toronto Press, 1995.

Strong-Boag, Veronica. *The Parliament of Women: The National Council of Women of Canada, 1893–1929*. Ottawa: National Museums of Canada, 1976.

Struthers, James. *The Limits of Affluence: Welfare in Ontario, 1920– 1970*. Toronto: University of Toronto Press, 1994.

Thomson, Jean Scott. *The Conditions of Female Labour in Ontario*. Toronto: Warwick, 1892.

Trofimenkoff, Susan Mann. 'One Hundred and Two Muffled Voices: Canada's Industrial Women in the 1880s.' In *Rethinking Canada: The Promise of Women's History*, ed. Veronica Strong-Boag and Anita Clair Fellman, 82–94. Toronto: Copp Clark Pitman, 1986.

Tucker, Eric. *Administering Danger in the Workplace: The Law and Politics of Occupational Health and Safety Regulation in Ontario, 1850–1914*. Toronto: University of Toronto Press, 1990.

Valverde, Mariana. *The Age of Light, Soap, and Water: Moral Reform in English Canada, 1885–1925*. Toronto: McClelland and Stewart, 1991.

Chapter 5   Resistance and Its Limits

Brandt, Gail Cuthbert. 'The Transformation of Women's Work in the Quebec Cotton Industry, 1920–1950.' In *The Character of Class Struggle: Essays in Canadian Working-Class History, 1850–1985*, ed. Bryan D. Palmer, 115–34. Toronto: McClelland and Stewart, 1986.

– '"Weaving It Together": Life Cycle and the Industrial Experience of Female Cotton Workers in Quebec, 1910–1950.' In *The Neglected Majority: Essays in Canadian Women's History*. Volume 2. Ed. Alison Prentice and Susan Mann Trofimenkoff, 160–73. Toronto: McClelland and Stewart, 1985.

Burr, Christina. *Spreading the Light: Work and Labour Reform in Late-Nineteenth-Century Toronto*. Toronto: University of Toronto Press, 1999.

Campbell, Marie. 'Sexism in British Columbia Trade Unions, 1900–1920.' In *In Her Own Right: Selected Essays on Women's History in British Columbia*, ed. Barbara Latham and Cathy Kess, 167–86. Victoria: Camosun College, 1980.

Creese, Gillian. 'The Politics of Dependence: Women, Work, and Unemployment in the Vancouver Labour Movement before World War II.' In *Class, Gender, and Region: Essays in Canadian Historical Sociology*, ed. Gregory S. Kealey, 121–42. St John's: Committee on Canadian Labour History, 1988.

Dubinsky, Karen. '"The Modern Chivalry": Women and Labor in Ontario, 1880–1891.' MA thesis, Carleton University, 1985.

Ferland, Jacques. '"In Search of the Unbound Prometheia": A Comparative View of Women's Activism in Two Quebec Industries, 1869–1908.' *Labour/Le Travail* 24 (Fall 1989): 11–45.

Frager, Ruth A. 'No Proper Deal: Women Workers and the Canadian Labour Movement, 1870–1940.' In *Union Sisters: Women in the Labour Movement*, ed. Linda Briskin and Lynda Yanz, 44–67. Toronto: Women's Press, 1983.

– *Sweatshop Strife: Class, Ethnicity, and Gender in the Jewish Labour Movement of Toronto, 1900–1939*. Toronto: University of Toronto Press, 1992.

Gorham, Deborah. 'Flora MacDonald Denison: Canadian Feminist.' In *A Not Unreasonable Claim: Women and Reform in Canada, 1880s–1920s*, ed. Linda Kealey, 47–70. Toronto: Women's Press, 1979.

Guildford, Janet. '"Separate Spheres": The Feminization of Public School Teaching in Nova Scotia, 1838–1880.' In *Separate Spheres: Women's Worlds in the 19th-Century Maritimes*, ed. Janet Guildford and Suzanne Morton, 119–45. Fredericton: Acadiensis Press, 1994.

Heap, Ruby, and Alison Prentice. '"The Outlook for Old Age Is Not Hopeful": The Struggle of Female Teachers over Pensions in Quebec, 1880–1914.' In *Quebec since 1800: Selected Readings*, ed. Michael D. Behiels, 313–40. Toronto: Irwin, 2002.

Heron, Craig. *The Canadian Labour Movement: A Short History*. Toronto: Lorimer, 1996.

– 'Factory Workers.' In *Labouring Lives: Work and Workers in Nineteenth-Century Ontario*, ed. Paul Craven, 479–590. Toronto: University of Toronto Press, 1995.

– ed. *The Workers' Revolt in Canada, 1917–1925*. Toronto: University of Toronto Press, 1998.

Howard, Irene. *The Struggle for Social Justice in British Columbia: Helena Gutteridge, the Unknown Reformer*. Vancouver: UBC Press, 1992.

Kealey, Gregory S., and Bryan D. Palmer. *Dreaming of What Might Be: The Knights of Labor in Ontario, 1880–1900*. Toronto: New Hogtown Press, 1987.

Kealey, Linda. *Enlisting Women for the Cause: Women, Labour, and the Left in Canada, 1890–1920*. Toronto: University of Toronto Press, 1998.

Kessler-Harris, Alice. '"Where Are the Organized Women Workers?"' *Feminist Studies* 3, nos. 1/2 (Fall 1975): 92–110.

Lavigne, Marie, and Jennifer Stoddart. 'Ouvrières et travailleuses montréalaises, 1900–1940.' In *Travailleuses et féministes: Les femmes dans la société québécoise*, ed. Marie Lavigne and Yolande Pinard, 99–113. Montreal: Boréal Express, 1983.

McClung, Nellie. *In Times Like These*. Toronto: University of Toronto Press, 1972 (originally published in 1915).

McPherson, Kathryn. *Bedside Matters: The Transformation of Canadian Nursing, 1900–1990*. Toronto: Oxford University Press, 1996.

Naylor, James. *The New Democracy: Challenging the Social Order in Industrial Ontario, 1914–1925*. Toronto: University of Toronto Press, 1991.

Newton, Janice. *The Feminist Challenge to the Canadian Left, 1900–1918*. Montreal and Kingston: McGill-Queen's University Press, 1995.

Roberts, Wayne. *Honest Womanhood: Feminism, Femininity and Class Consciousness among Toronto Working Women, 1893 to 1914*. Toronto: New Hogtown Press, 1976.

Rosenthal, Star. 'Union Maids: Organized Women Workers in Vancouver, 1900–1915.' *BC Studies* 41 (Spring 1979): 36–55.

Sangster, Joan. 'The 1907 Bell Telephone Strike: Organizing Women Workers.' *Labour/Le Travailleur* 3 (1978): 109–30.

– 'Canadian Working Women.' In *Lectures in Canadian Labour and Working-Class History*, ed. W.J.C. Cherwinski and Gregory S. Kealey, 59–78. St John's: Committee on Canadian Labour History, 1985.

– *Dreams of Equality: Women on the Canadian Left, 1920–1950*. Toronto: McClelland and Stewart, 1989.

– *Earning Respect: The Lives of Working Women in Small-Town Ontario, 1920–1960*. Toronto: University of Toronto Press, 1995.

Staton, Pat. 'Validating Women's Work through "Grass-Roots" History: Bertha Adkins – A Case Study.' *Canadian Woman Studies* 7, no. 4 (1986): 82–6.

Steedman, Mercedes. *Angels of the Workplace: Women and the Construction of Gender Relations in the Canadian Clothing Industry, 1890–1940*. Toronto: Oxford University Press, 1997.

Struthers, James. '"Lord Give Us Men": Women and Social Work in English Canada, 1918–1953.' Canadian Historical Association *Historical Papers* (1983): 96–112.

Conclusion

Patrias, Carmela, and Ruth A. Frager. '"This Is Our Country, These Are Our Rights": Minorities and the Origins of

Ontario's Human Rights Campaigns.' *Canadian Historical Review* 82, no. 1 (2001): 1–35.

Phillips, Paul, and Erin Phillips. *Women and Work: Inequality in the Canadian Labour Market.* Toronto: Lorimer, 1993.

Prentice, Alison, Paula Bourne, Gail Cuthbert Brandt, Beth Light, Wendy Mitchinson, Naomi Black. *Canadian Women: A History.* 2nd ed. Toronto: Harcourt Brace, 1996.

Sangster, Joan. 'Doing Two Jobs: The Wage-Earning Mother, 1945–70.' In *A Diversity of Women: Ontario, 1945–1980*, ed. Joy Parr, 98–134. Toronto: University of Toronto Press, 1995.

Tillotson, Shirley. 'Human Rights Law as Prism: Women's Organizations, Unions, and Ontario's Female Employees Fair Remuneration Act, 1951.' *Canadian Historical Review* 72, no. 4 (1991): 532–57.

Index

THEMES IN CANADIAN HISTORY

Editors:
Colin Coates 2003–
Craig Heron 1997–
Franca Iacovetta 1997–1999